Writing Our Communities

http://kcac.kennesaw.edu

The Keeping and Creating American Communities (KCAC) project of the Kennesaw Mountain Writing Project is a program initially funded by the National Endowment for the Humanities and supported by the National Writing Project. The KCAC project has brought together teacher-researchers, their students, and community members in inquiry and writing to recover stories from the past, participate actively in civic life, and create future communities to which all Americans can belong. The interdisciplinary curriculum of the KCAC project serves students and teachers from elementary school through university.

Writing Our Communities

Local Learning and Public Culture

Edited by

Dave Winter
Henry W. Grady High School, Atlanta

Sarah Robbins
Kennesaw State University

Associate editors:
Peggy Maynard Corbett, Mimi Dyer, Patsy Hamby, Stacie Janecki,
Linda Hadley Stewart, and Leslie M. Walker

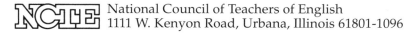
National Council of Teachers of English
1111 W. Kenyon Road, Urbana, Illinois 61801-1096

National Writing Project
2105 Bancroft Way #1042, Berkeley, California 94720-1042

Staff Editor: Bonny Graham

Interior Design: Doug Burnett

Cover Design: Pat Mayer

NCTE Stock Number: 59206

Library of Congress Cataloging-in-Publication Data
Writing our communities : local learning and public culture / edited by Dave Winter, Sarah Robbins.
    p. cm.
  Includes bibliographical references.
  ISBN 0-8141-5920-6 (pbk)
  1. Community—Study and teaching—United States—Case studies.
2. Community life—United States—Study and teaching—Case studies.
3. United States—History, Local—Study and teaching—Case studies.
4. English language—Composition and exercises—Study and teaching.
5. Lesson planning. I. Winter, Dave, 1967– II. Robbins, Sarah.
  HM756.W755 2005
  307' . 071'073—dc22

                                                                2004021097

To our students, whose enthusiasm for and excellence in conducting community studies made this book a reality

Permission Acknowledgments

Some of the material in this book appeared originally—and in the case of a few passages, still appears—on the KCAC project Web site. In particular, we excerpt descriptions of themes for the KCAC program with permission of the Kennesaw Mountain Writing Project.

For the photograph of Jimmy Carter, his mother, and his sister in our Cultivating Homelands image, we draw from a photograph appearing in President Carter's memoir, *An Hour before Daylight: Memories of a Rural Boyhood.* © Carter Family Collection, courtesy of the Jimmy Carter Library and Museum.

The image of Sequoyah used in the logo for our Recovering Displaced Heritages theme is courtesy of the National Portrait Gallery at the Smithsonian Institution in Washington, D.C., accession number NPG.79.174. The image comes from a painting by Henry Inman, which in turn is a copy of a now-destroyed painting by Charles Bird King.

Carrie P. Walls's "Children's Exchange," published in the November 1886 *Spelman Messenger,* is reprinted with permission of the Spelman College Archives.

Contents

Preface

Dear Colleague,

We all know that look, that detached, squinty, glazed-over stare that says, "I'll do this activity (or I won't do it), but I'm doing it for you, to meet your expectations, to complete your assignment, to get your grade." It's a universal student look; teachers get it at every level, from elementary to college students, from the most resistant learners to the most motivated—whatever the subject. We fear that oftentimes the problem isn't with our students: it's with our approach to teaching them.

How can students create rather than regurgitate knowledge that matters to them? How can they interact meaningfully with the community around them? How can the classroom become a real community, not a contrived one in which teacher and student are performing for each other? We, the teacher-researchers of the Keeping and Creating American Communities project, began our inquiry hoping to find answers to these questions. We believe that students need to engage the multiple communities that surround them and also that those communities benefit from the energy and enthusiasm that students can bring to active citizenship, where citizenship means recovering, critiquing, and actively engaging the world around them. Once teachers encourage their students to research and to write about community, the classroom comes alive in wonderful and unexpected ways. As students learn more about the communities around them, they discover how important keeping community ties and creating new ones can be.

The lessons contained in this volume represent our attempts to bring community into our classrooms and our classrooms to the community. Crossing local, regional, national, and virtual borders as well, these lessons are organized primarily by how they fit into the larger curriculum. The first section includes strategies for introducing writing-intensive community studies in minilessons that last less than a class period. The second section extends these strategies to daily lessons or multiple, linked activities. The third section includes fully developed research units organized around core principles for studying community life. The final section presents lessons that build on those principles after they have been established in the classroom. The lessons in this section represent extended projects that became the primary course objectives, for both the teachers who assigned them and the students who completed them.

You will find that these lessons are transportable across grade level, student ability, and discipline. They have already been shared, adapted, and implemented by the diverse group of teachers who constitute our own community. We invite you and your students to join us in the enterprise of keeping and creating American communities.

Patsy Hamby
Sarah Robbins
Linda Hadley Stewart
Rozlyn T. Truss
Leslie M. Walker
Dave Winter

Acknowledgments

This book inviting teachers to build curricula around communities understandably is indebted to many members of our own project community and to others who have helped us grow.

Because our writing grew out of a grant-funded curriculum project, colleagues who contributed to that program also shaped this publication. We are grateful to the many talented facilitators who have worked with us in summer institutes and school-year continuity events during the grant-funded phase of our program. We hope they will see exciting traces of their teaching in the lessons shared here. In particular, we acknowledge the ongoing involvement of our National Advisory Board: Randy Bass, Thadious Davis, Paul Lauter, Cristine Levenduski, Diana Mitchell, and David Scobey. Each led study sessions, but they also stayed connected to the KCAC project throughout its initial inquiry and curriculum development phases.

We thank our primary funder, the National Endowment for the Humanities—especially our program officers at the NEH, Janet Edwards and Robert Sayers, whose guidance has been invigorating and nurturing. We appreciate other major supporters, including the National Writing Project, Kennesaw State University, the Cracker Barrel Foundation, and many school districts in Georgia and around the country. Spelman College's archivist, Taronda Spencer, provided invaluable support for our research into the institution's early history and assisted us with permissions to use material from the collection for our Web site and in classroom teaching approaches described here. We thank the many members of local organizations (historical societies and theater groups, PTAs and corporations)—as well as the countless individual community members—who have graciously given time, advice, knowledge, and resources to our enterprise. We also would like to thank our three pilot teachers—Judy Bebelaar in California, Sharon Bishop in Nebraska, and Barbara Howry in Oklahoma—for their continued commitment to disseminating the work of this project through their writing and their willingness to share it with the National Writing Project sites in their hometowns.

During the preparation of our manuscript, we received expert guidance from senior editor Zarina Hock and staff editor Bonny Graham at NCTE, from Amy Bauman of the National Writing Project, and from a cadre of insightful reviewers. Their enthusiasm and support for the project encouraged us when we needed it most. A few of our project team members merit special thanks here for editorial assistance. Sharon Bishop, Traci Blanchard, LeeAnn Lands, Linda Templeton, and Rozlyn Truss supported the associate editors' preparation of the Curricular Crossings text, a key feature of this collection. Landon Brown II, Patsy Hamby, Ed Hullender, Steve Jones, Deborah Mitchell, Kiran Narker, Diane Shearer, Scott Smoot, and Sylvia Martinez Spruill contributed much to our work, both through their ongoing KCAC participation and in writing they did for related KCAC performances and publications, such as our Web site. Oscar Bryan and Peggy Corbett conscientiously assisted with editing chores as graduate student interns. KCAC project co-director Mimi Dyer generously aided our editing.

Special thanks go to all the students who have been authors in our classrooms. Space considerations made it impossible to include many, many fine pieces of writing of which we are very proud. We hope readers will visit our Web site (http://kcac.kennesaw.edu) to see additional examples of student writing, lessons, and teachers' reflections from our classrooms. The artifacts here represent just a few samples of the body of writing that teachers and students have crafted together while "keeping and creating American communities."

Introduction: Building Communities of Learning—An Invitation to Teachers

Sarah Robbins

Individualism has been a central value of American democracy, but community building plays an equally important role in sustaining a society—one of the major goals of education in any era. With that aim in mind, this book presents classroom-tested approaches for interdisciplinary, writing-based exploration of American communities. As colleagues from the Keeping and Creating American Communities (KCAC) project indicate in the preface, all of us involved in this particular curriculum program have benefited enormously from having a chance to study and refine our teaching while simultaneously researching and writing—with our students—about the communities in which we live. Throughout this collaboration, we have drawn on concepts of literacy use that balance a commitment to individual expression with an understanding that writing also reflects and potentially contributes to community development. As we have outlined in a companion volume of teacher inquiry narratives, *Writing America: Classroom Literacy and Public Engagement,* our participation in the Keeping and Creating American Communities program has changed our teaching and, in many cases, changed the places where we live. In addition, through this shared experience we have learned particular teaching approaches that other educators committed to community-based learning can adapt to their own settings.

This collection of lessons represents one of our efforts to share what we have learned with other educators. Throughout the program, sharing both our struggles and our successes has been a central feature of our work, one tremendously enriched by the inclusion of teachers from around the United States, from all grade levels (elementary through college), from a variety of disciplines, and from a wide array of settings (urban, rural, suburban, and transitional). We envision our audience for this collection as coming, like our own diverse group, from a range of classrooms and teaching students of varying ages in many disciplinary contexts.

Although the chance to be part of this team has been unusually rewarding, the work we've done can be adapted to any setting. Indeed, this collection has been conceived and arranged to show that anyone who believes in the power of interdisciplinary research and writing can develop engaging approaches for studying community life along with students.

As a model for generating curriculum, Keeping and Creating American Communities has drawn on several core principles, which we outline and illustrate in more detail on our project Web site (http:// kcac.kennesaw.edu). First, we believe that writing can be a crucial tool for creating communities, in the classroom and beyond. We affirm that collaboration is essential to both keeping and creating community, and that students of all ages, working with teachers in any discipline, can engage in meaningful, community-based research that has authentic, publicly significant goals and outcomes. For us, in fact, perhaps the most "authentic" research is inquiry aimed at participating in—and even shaping—community life. We invite students to become analysts of their own communities by studying a variety of primary texts, ranging from photographs to archival documents, from public history sites to oral histories. We believe this kind of research is powerful in part because it recognizes ways in which even the smallest local communities (such as classrooms, neighborhoods, hometowns) continually reshape themselves in relation to larger ones—the regions we live in, the nation we aspire to be, the international networks to which we all increasingly belong. So that our students can become proactive citizens, we design curriculum inviting them to recover and interpret (i.e., to "keep") and to "create" community texts of their own. This book provides other teachers with some tools for doing the same.

Using Lessons on Community in Your Classroom

On one level, the lessons in this collection are indeed "lesson plans." They outline the steps that individual teachers have followed in their classrooms with real students. They include samples of student work— examples you may give to your own students to imitate *and to critique.*

The latter goal (to critique the student texts here) is particularly important. The classroom writing included here comes from a range of learning occasions. As artifacts of classroom culture in action, these texts are not all intended to serve as models of ideal work. Certainly many of the pieces are outstanding, and student writers (as well as teachers) will see techniques worth emulating. But many of the student texts in this collection come from writing-to-learn activities, not extended writing-to-publish enterprises, and we purposely include such pieces as they were originally drafted (not in revised form) to illustrate that much of the community-building writing done in classrooms can be exploratory—unpolished yet productive as a critical-thinking tool. One rationale we have for publishing such texts—writing that was not originally produced with publication in mind—is to open up the walls of our classrooms to other teachers, especially busy educators in a range of disciplines who may think they can't teach writing because they don't have the time or expertise to guide student work through revision and editing stages. In fact, we hope one way that students and teachers will use the sample classroom texts here is to consider together how some of the "unfinished" pieces might be extended, revised, and polished into more formal products.

The lesson plans themselves range from short learning activities that take up less than a class period, to mini-units taught over several class sessions, to extended units and ambitious group projects. Without having any formal introduction to the KCAC program, you will be able to browse through this collection and choose particular activities that would be fun—and challenging—to try with students.

Although we present our lessons in clusters based on the approximate amount of time we planned to give to them (ranging from one class period to many weeks), in practice these divisions are somewhat artificial. Often an activity that was originally envisioned as taking a single class period grew organically into a more extended learning experience. In such cases, we have tried in the reflection section of the chapter to retrace that extension process, partly to model how teachers' professional growth is incremental, gradually building on what might initially be rather small-scale experiments.

Enjoy experimenting with our ideas and adapting them to your own setting. To encourage you to reshape individual lessons for your own teaching context, we have included examples of possible cross-level and cross-disciplinary modifications. You will also notice, in the reflections section at the close of each entry, that KCAC teachers themselves often redesigned their curriculum dramatically after analyzing their work the first time around.

Reflecting on Community-Based Teaching

On another level, beyond simply using individual activities in this book, we hope you will think about our anthology as a collective story about a group of educators who joined together to study their own teaching and their students' learning. On this level, each of the components in the book's individual entries conveys something important that we as a group have learned about the power of community-based teaching.

Perhaps most important, we have learned that reflecting on our teaching makes us better teachers and that written reflection can be an especially powerful stimulus for refining our work. Most of us were in the habit of critiquing our teaching before we began to concentrate on community studies. But writing analytically about our work for this publication and for our Web site has underscored the enormous impact that shared, written reflection can have on teaching. Each of the reflections you will read here was drafted by one teacher but read by others in our group, who provided editorial feedback and support for more analysis. While revisions of the lesson plans themselves were generally focused simply on making the process clearer and on ensuring that they provided an accurate picture of what originally happened in the classroom, revisions of the reflections often pushed our thinking in new directions or helped us interpret our work as educators more deeply and critically.

One way, then, that reading through this collection can support your professional growth is by encouraging you to reflect on and write about your own classroom and to share your written reflections with other educators. This practice of sustained, collaborative reflection has been especially productive for our own community of teacher-learners. We have written *to* one another on a listserv, written *for* one another in short description and analysis papers during our project continuity days, and written *about* ourselves and our students. These records of learning, like the individual teacher reflections following each of the lessons in this book, represent one way we have built community—and a way through which we hope you will join our community too, by reading our stories and writing your own interpretations of your classroom.

Like our reflections, the student writing samples in this collection are intended to serve a double purpose. Besides providing individual examples for how-to assignments, the student writing, taken as a whole, emphasizes several things we have learned about community-based teaching. Should you choose to read through the student writing as texts separate from the lesson plans, we think you will gradually develop a strong sense of the values and principles that have guided our work in community studies.

First of all, you will notice a rich diversity in the kinds of writing students in our classrooms have been producing, and you will see that this writing often includes or interacts with nonprint media such as photography or art, speeches or public spaces. You will also see that much of our students' writing is grounded in actively researching where they live. This research may involve using a variety of nontraditional approaches and analytical tools from multiple disciplines. It certainly will allow for creative publication opportunities and for frequent celebrations of student writing as a community-building agent, both in the classroom and beyond.

The way we referred to these student pieces during the assembly and editing process for this book offers a revealing window into our beliefs about the power of writing communities within school settings. By describing the student writing as "artifacts," we are signaling that we see our classrooms as significant cultural spaces, where records of community life are constantly being made through students' composing processes. We believe such artifacts should be treasured, so including student contributions in this collection signifies that commitment. By naming our student work "texts" instead of "assignments," we are reminding ourselves that student writing itself should be an object of study just as important as those heavy textbooks issued by our schools. Student writing seen in these terms is contributing to the formation of a living culture—one inside the classroom but also reaching beyond into larger American communities. Thus, besides seeing the student writing here as a guide to using our lesson plans, we hope you will read our students' works all together as a cumulative record of community formation. Taken as a whole, the student work gathered here embodies much that we have learned about "creating American communities," especially the ability of writing to contribute to that enterprise.

Like the reflections and student writing in each section of this collection, our lesson plans can be read all together as a distinct narrative. While we are excited to imagine you trying out individual lessons and adapting the longer units, we also hope you will think about the lessons as identifying basic concepts that can be even more generative for your classroom. When you read the lessons as a collection designed by educators who were working as a team, you will notice common practices, shared beliefs, and recurring strategies that are guiding our teaching across all levels and disciplines. When you draw on those patterns conceptually, you will find yourself developing your own lessons, imagining the student writing those lessons can generate, and reflecting on the ways that writing can help students understand and create community culture. You may soon find yourself taking notes, as we have done, about the meaning of events in your classroom as an evolving community. National Writing Project teacher-consultant Diana Mitchell's closing remarks are especially helpful in this regard.

Making More Connections

We hope you will visit the Keeping and Creating American Communities Web site, where we have many more lesson plans, additional reflections on our learning experiences, and fuller descriptions of our guiding principles. In addition, we hope you'll contact us directly at kmwp@kennesaw.edu if you have questions about our work. Finally, we hope you'll connect with the National Writing Project (NWP) location nearest your home. All of the teachers involved in the original KCAC project team are affiliated with one of the NWP's many sites around the country, with the majority of us coming from Georgia sites in the Atlanta area. Because the principles guiding our KCAC research and teaching have been grounded in our NWP experience, if you find the teaching approaches represented in this book appealing, you would also find much of value in the National Writing Project's ongoing program.

Thematic Strands for Studying Community

KCAC Project Teachers and Amy Meadows

We and our students have studied ways in which American communities are formed in various times and places by drawing on a cluster of themes. These themes originally guided the inquiry of teacher participants at summer institutes and in academic-year inquiry teams. Later, we adapted the themes for teaching in a wide range of settings and disciplines. The following list identifies the basic content of each theme, the first two of which focus on community-oriented action and the next three of which emphasize the power of place:

- Reclaiming Displaced Heritages—recovering aspects of history and local culture that could be undervalued or misunderstood by future generations

- Educating for Citizenship—developing learning approaches that prepare community members for active engagement in American democracy

- Cultivating Homelands—shaping the natural environment and drawing on it for support while honoring traditions of rural life

- Building Cities—analyzing urban spaces that represent and promote community values in particular historical periods

- Shifting Landscapes, Converging Peoples—reconfiguring contemporary suburban landscapes and social practices to balance a region's local heritage with newcomers' cultural contributions

Because we have found these themes to be so productive for student learning, one of the organizational plans for this book (as seen in the table of contents on the inside front cover) highlights their role as organizing tools for teaching. With that in mind, following is an overview of ways we have used each theme.

Drawn from the program Web site (http://kcac.kennesaw.edu).

Reclaiming Displaced Heritages

Typically, when studying community through this thematic lens, teachers and students identify a particular occasion when members of a community have been disenfranchised in ways that may have suppressed or obscured records of their cultural heritage. Students read literature associated with such groups' communal stories, visit public history sites,

Reclaiming Displaced Heritages

study changes in the local landscape, and gather additional records of cultural experience (such as oral histories, photographs, public documents).

In Georgia, for example, our initial application of this theme involved reexamining the Cherokee Removal, including studying the causes leading up to the historical event, its effects on the land and social practices in northwest Georgia, and its impact on members of the Cherokee Nation, from the 1800s until today. Participants read texts such as Diane Glancy's *Pushing the Bear* and Robert Conley's *Mountain Windsong* alongside primary historical documents from the era of the Removal. They visited sites such as New Echota (the former capital of the Cherokee Nation), and they contributed to the writing of a play about events in Georgia leading up to the Removal.

Given this initial focus for our work with this theme, on our Web site and in this book we have used an image of Sequoyah to designate this body of our work. Sequoyah, who was born to the daughter of a Cherokee chief and a Virginia fur trader in the village of Tuskeegee in 1776, developed the Cherokee writing system in 1809 after moving to Georgia to flee the encroachment of white settlers. In 1821 the Cherokee Nation officially adopted the system, which helped lead to the publication of the first Native American newspaper, *The Cherokee Phoenix.*

Educating for Citizenship

This theme considers how various groups have tried to use education as a way of claiming a place in American culture. At the same time, it invites teachers to educate today's students for informed, proactive citizenship.

For example, while using this theme, teachers in our project group studied the early history of Spelman College as an example of collaboration between blacks and whites to create an empowering educational institution for African Americans in the decades after the Civil War. Team members collected oral histories and archival materials, including turn-of-the-century copies of *The Spelman Messenger,* a bulletin about college students and graduates. Along the way, team members considered how students' awareness of educational opportunities often taken for granted today could shape their involvement in citizenship issues in the future.

Educating for Citizenship

As a logo to mark this theme, we chose an image of the Georgia State Capitol Building, dedicated on July 4, 1889. The capitol building is the center of the State Capitol Complex in Atlanta.

Cultivating Homelands

This theme delves into rural communities, seeking ways to honor their traditions and complexities. Teachers and students research records of rural life, such as landmarks (cemeteries, barns, churches, historic homes), documents (land grant deeds, archival photographs, family Bibles), and social practices such as regional festivals. While preservationist energies drive much of the work around this theme, participants

Cultivating Homelands

also question why some aspects of their communities' past have received more attention than others, and what familiar narratives of local life need to be expanded or revised—and how.

Our first application of this theme explored the heritage of farm communities in Georgia, especially in the early twentieth century. Reading Raymond Andrews's *The Last Radio Baby* and former president Jimmy Carter's *An Hour before Daylight*, the group traced similarities and differences in these vivid narratives about rural experiences. Our inquiry into the histories of local places often promoted grassroots collaborations with citizens' groups, sometimes leading to the renovation of neglected sites. These efforts taught us that chronicling parts of a rural community's history can help develop communities of critical thinkers and informed preservationists.

To delineate this theme on our Web site and in this book, we have used a photograph from Jimmy Carter's memoir, *An Hour before Daylight.* A young Carter poses with his mother and sister in rural Plains, Georgia, circa 1933. The son of a farmer who owned land, Carter grew up among tenant sharecroppers, often working alongside them to harvest the cash crops of peanuts and cotton for his family. His book, like research done through this theme by students and teachers, honors the continuing influence of rural heritage on American culture.

Building Cities

To study community through this thematic lens, teachers and students focus on a particular period when the identity of a city in their region was being constructed to reflect a vision of that community as distinctively American. Learners using this theme typically visit urban buildings and neighborhoods, interview longtime residents, retrace key developments in architecture and urban planning, and identify ways in which political, social, and economic forces converged to affect a city's way of life.

Building Cities

The Georgia team initially explored this theme by reimagining Atlanta as a cultural, corporate center, with emphasis on ways that 1970s–1990s civic leaders tried to move the city from being a regional center to having a national and international presence. Teachers read Frederick Allen's *Atlanta Rising: The Invention of an International City, 1946–1996*, took an architectural walking tour of downtown, visited urban museums, and began to gather family stories about life in the city of Atlanta. Studying Dolores Hayden's *The Power of Place* and Paul Fleischman's *Seedfolks* helped teachers consider how they and their students might contribute to the culture of the city through writing and new kinds of landmark making.

As a logo for this theme, we selected images of several Atlanta landmarks that would resonate outside our own region. Pictured clockwise from the top in the logo are John Portman's Westin Peachtree Plaza Hotel, at one time the tallest hotel in the western hemisphere and home to the three-story revolving Sun Dial Restaurant; the former Winecoff Hotel, site of a 1946 fire that killed a record 119 people, spurring hotel fire safety measures nationwide; and the Carnegie Building, completed in 1925 as the Wynne-Claughton Building and hailed then for its landmark exterior design.

Shifting Landscapes, Converging Peoples

The Shifting Landscapes, Converging Peoples theme explores how the rapidly changing landscapes of contemporary suburbia can be reconfigured to achieve a productive balance between the native and the newcomers' cultural contributions. Teachers and students actively interpret changing social spaces, such as restaurants, public buildings, and shopping centers; cultural events, such as fairs, homecomings, and ethnic celebrations; public policies, including planning and zoning ordinances; and oral histories that both keep the old way of life and help create the new.

To begin their study of suburbia, the Georgia KCAC team studied Kenneth T. Jackson's *Crabgrass Frontier: The Suburbanization of the United States* and listened to the National Public Radio oral memoirs of Carmen Agra Deedy on *Growing Up Cuban in Decatur, Georgia.* They also became avid readers of their local newspapers, tracking recurring stories about immigrants' experiences, innovations in suburban lifestyle, and issues associated with sprawl (e.g., traffic, endangered natural resources). They took walking tours of Atlanta

Shifting Landscapes, Converging Peoples

suburbs. Students interviewed contractors about how subdivisions are designed and built, used digital cameras to record the rapid changes in the suburban landscape, and talked with both longtime residents and newcomers about their views on life in the outskirts of Atlanta.

The logo for this theme records a scene familiar to suburban life all over the United States today. Two soccer players reflect the growing diversity in suburban public schools like Wheeler High in Cobb County, Georgia, where this photo was taken.

I Introductory Activities

1 Sharing Stories to Build Community

Linda Hadley Stewart
Kennesaw State University, Kennesaw, Georgia

Overview

Seeking a warm-up activity that reflected the KCAC emphasis on storytelling as a way of understanding and composing history, I asked my students to write about a memorable tree-climbing experience (or related activity, such as building a tree house or creating a backyard "club"). Brannen's paper is the result of a writing activity I assigned the first day of our English composition class to be read aloud to the entire class at the following meeting. This type of writing activity would, I hoped, reveal and validate the different ways we tell stories, begin to create community through describing a shared experience, and prepare the students for reading Raymond Andrews's memoir *The Last Radio Baby,* a KCAC Summer Institute selection.

This brief assignment was a trial balloon that yielded some significant results. Brannen's paper is a paradigm for the many papers that emerged from this assignment. I chose his paper to include because his essay uncannily evoked several KCAC themes. When he speaks of white flight, he touches on our theme of Shifting Landscapes, Converging Peoples. His description of the removal of the landmark jet evokes the Building Cities thematic content. I realized that

> The English composition course is the second in a sequence of required general education courses at Kennesaw State University in Kennesaw, Georgia. Once a small, rural community, Kennesaw is now considered a suburb of metro Atlanta. The university is primarily a commuter campus serving nearly 18,000 students. This course, limited to 25 students, focuses on writing and research. Many of the students are from rural and suburban northwest Georgia; a significant number, however, are international students from countries such as Nigeria, Guatemala, Bulgaria, or Brazil. Student ages range widely because many are returning to Kennesaw to complete or begin their college careers as adults.

Shifting Landscapes, Converging Peoples

the assignment had elicited concepts and ideas that KCAC recognizes and explicitly names. These principles, fused with teaching practices (e.g., valuing storytelling), have galvanized my students' writing and thinking.

Brannen's paper meanders through the suburban streets on Brannen's return home from military duty as he describes the streets both past and present. His paper is laden with historical observations and personal memories. In so many ways, Brannen's writing evokes the work and the value of community-based inquiry. His narrative artfully fuses home and place, memory and history, the personal and the public. His paper begs the question, "What was there before?" His former address, "Six-One-Nine Camelia Circle," becomes present as he describes the rotting remains of the tree his father removed "to make room for his old Volvo."

His writing, like that of many of his classmates who shared their brief memoirs, reveals the twine of personal memory with cultural history, much as Raymond Andrews's memoir reveals the history of rural Georgia in the early 1900s. This initial writing assignment was a wedge into our later exploration of and writing about the communities around us. Through this initial assignment, students began to validate storytelling, recognizing how culture and history are at work in their personal lives.

Instructional Sequence

For this course-opening activity, students arrive in class ready to read their journal entries to the class. The assignment is given as homework the previous class, and students are aware that they will be reading their writing aloud to the entire class. The writing prompt invites them to tell a story about the first time they climbed a tree or to adapt the topic to a similar outdoor experience. When asked to volunteer, students have shown a willingness to read, which is surprising since this must be a somewhat high-anxiety task so early in the semester.

I ask everyone to have journals out and note details, passages, ways of telling stories, subject matter, or other observations. They are encouraged to listen carefully and write down their observations because they will be posting them in response to a prompt on an electronic discussion board.

At the end of class, after listening to their comments and insights, I summarize particular rhetorical strategies, note different motivations for tree climbing, underscore the cultural aspects of their personal stories, and emphasize much of what the students have already shared.

To extend this brief assignment, I have students post online observations about the class discussion. We brainstorm possible research or writing activities that could emerge from the various narratives and then compile a class list of these activities. Most important, we have built a sound foundation for the semester by sharing and validating many ways of telling stories.

Student Artifact

Journal Entry—Tree Climbing

I make the left turn from Green Street onto Pleasant Hill Road after a night of delayed and finally diminished anticipation. I had hoped my first night back home would culminate elsewhere, but the only guest that accompanies me is the slight fragrance of alcohol and cigarette smoke. I follow Pleasant Hill about three quarters of a mile, making a sharp right turn past Sewell Circle Park. A static model of an old Air Force jet once decorated the edge of the park, but the "powers that be" dismantled and relocated it to a different side of town. This is the "old neighborhood."

When I was younger most of the inhabitants of this area were white. As I aged, they changed and the neighborhood darkened. I witnessed "white flight" before I ever knew there was a term to describe it. Families began moving southward to the country, where newer homes, schools, and less diversity existed. About the same time that whites in the neighborhood began flying south, the jet at Sewell Circle Park took off and landed in another park. The jet was a tribute to Robbins Air Force Base, which supplies 20,000 civilian jobs to central Georgia. My father was one of those employees. Apparently, the new inhabitants of our old neighborhood were unworthy of having the jet in their neighborhood. I passed the park and made a left onto Camelia Circle. I drove past the home of my old friend Charles Ranger.

When we were five, Charlie's mom heard me call Charlie a few select names during a fight the two of us were having. Charlie and I were no longer allowed to play together. She didn't know I learned the words from her son. I was disappointed about losing my friend, but the incident only supported my belief that his mom was crazy. She looked like a homely, red-haired Cher. Charlie once told me his mom and dad showered together to save water. It was 1983, Reagan was president; the only thing America cared about conserving was nuclear weaponry. To hell with water!

Four or five houses down from Charlie's house is Six-One-Nine Camelia Circle. The first address I ever learned. It is my old house. We moved in 1985, but my father still owns it. It no longer looks like it did when I lived there. The red brick was replaced with some type of plastic or poly-whatever-you-have-it siding years ago. A large evergreen once flanked the right side. It bombarded the front yard with blue-green meteors. In the hands of my older sisters they became flying projectiles, bullets, or missiles, just a euphemism for one more item to throw at Brannen and make his life miserable.

But if the tree created a source of misery, it also provided a means of escape. The trunk opened up like a stairwell so that a small child, like myself, could easily climb the branches. These trees tend to grow out rather than up, so my fear of heights was never able to take advantage of my fear of sisters. It was easy to find a place to lie for hours, surrounded by the tree's fruit. Carpenter ants tickled the little white hairs on my arms. They were the "good" ants because they never bit. It is difficult to remember the texture of the limbs or the trunk. I mostly remember the berries.

The tree no longer stands by the right side of my old home. My father felled it before we moved. He needed to make room for his old Volvo. The tree blocked a potential parking spot on the side of the house. It became a victim of its own random, stubborn nature. It grew in the wrong place, and would be moved only by force. The only remains are rotting if they haven't already. Gone like childhood, unearthed only by returning children who are curious about their memories.

—Brannen

Teacher Reflection

Let me offer some background about why I chose this particular assignment. It was the result of a class conversation the previous semester when one of my students mentioned climbing a magnolia tree and her classmates showed great interest in her story. Realizing this was an activity they all shared, I asked them to tell me their tree stories, and I left the class mulling over the various kinds of trees they so clearly described and the different motivations for climbing trees—for sanctuary, for competition, for solace, for companionship, for a better view, and simply because "everyone else was climbing it." The following semester I decided to start with this activity, explaining to my class why I had chosen it: because their predecessors had shown me that it was a shared activity, one that a student called "a national pastime."

My students' tree stories surprise me with their range and unsolicited vivid description. Students describe mango trees and magnolia trees; reveal their competitive and ambitious response to a challenge;

discover a fear of heights; narrate a formula plot; call on metaphor; re-member family relationships; celebrate imagination; and delve into their personal histories. Students repeatedly express surprise at how a simi-lar, shared experience can produce such an array of writing styles and subject matter. And they begin to connect their personal histories with cultural practices, examining their stories in a fuller context within their new classroom community.

Trees are deeply personal, but they are political, environmental, cultural, poetic, literary, and historical as well. Think clear-cutting, the Survivor Tree at the Oklahoma City National Memorial, trees as sign-posts for Cherokee along the Trail of Tears, to name a few. This brief tree-climbing warm-up assignment is a good springboard for writing and research activities such as reading newspaper articles; connecting to poetry; completing a scientific observation; interviewing a tree farmer or a land developer; or visiting trees that function as icons. This assign-ment works as an introductory or journal response to any novel or lit-erary work with a tree as a central or minor trope (e.g., *A Separate Peace, Beloved, Their Eyes Were Watching God*). Or, to encourage us to think as citizens, as a prelude to planting a tree for conservation or memoriali-zation. I've learned much from listening to my students' tree stories, and they provide our classroom community with rich material to begin a semester of writing and research.

Community ✛ Crossings

Suggestions on how you might adapt this lesson for a different classroom setting

- This activity could be used with any shared cultural experience, such as public transportation stories in an urban setting, vacation stories, bicycle stories, etc. Using a common writing prompt reveals the different ways stories are told even as it creates community within the class. This activity could be extended by having students identify similar stories in the media (e.g., cartoons, films, television shows, news) and analyze the various ways of sharing these stories.

- Younger students could illustrate their stories and then tell them to the class. Another option would be for students to create an illustrated storyboard of their narratives, either independently or collaboratively. Such storyboards could include captions.

- Another way to build community early in the course is to have students construct a "life map." Students choose five to seven defining moments or life stories to represent graphically, such as a poster, a computer-generated representation, or other format. Each student presents his or her life map to the class, explaining the significance of each event. Sharing these life maps helps students recognize how much they have in common with others who might, on the surface, seem very different. The activity also helps to foster a safe and supportive learning environment for classrooms of all levels. For other variations of this lesson, see Deborah Mitchell and Traci Blanchard's "Critical Reading, Imaginative Writing and the Me Montage" in the Extended Lesson Treatments section of Classroom Resources on the KCAC Web site (http://kcac.kennesaw.edu/).

2 Making the Classroom Our Place

Leslie M. Walker
Campbell High School, Smyrna, Georgia

Overview

Based on the philosophy that the classroom is a community in itself, and valuing the places each student comes from, this lesson is appropriate as a first-day-of-class activity to begin to foster a sense of community in this new place we inhabit together. This one-day

School: Campbell High School
City: Smyrna, Georgia
Grade level: 10
Discipline: literature/composition
School setting: urban
Number of students: 30
Students in school: 2,000

lesson allows the students to reflect on where they live and to consider what places are most significant to them.

Objective

Students will read *My Place,* written by Nadia Wheatley and illustrated by Donna Rawlins. The book presents the history of the Botany Bay region of Australia as told through the voices and drawings of fictional children. Each young voice relates his or her perception of the neigh-

Educating for Citizenship

Cultivating Homelands

borhood at varying times in words and through a map illustrating their perceptions of place at that moment. Each new narrator transports the reader back a generation. Although the book is intended for younger readers, it works exceedingly well in high school because perceptive readers, by juxtaposing the maps and narrators, can piece together the evolution of the town, its culture, its economy, and its demographics. Sometimes what the young narrators don't see is more important than what they do. After reading and discussing the text, the students will draw a map of their own neighborhood (following the pattern set by the narrators in *My Place*), visualizing what they see within a one-mile radius of their homes and labeling places they consider most significant.

Instructional Sequence

Have students read *My Place,* either by assigning each student a decade/chapter to read aloud or by allowing volunteers to read. Note the significance of the last chapter and the line, "I belong to this place." Lead discussion on the difference between "belonging" to a place and "owning" a place. Provide the students with markers and white paper and have them draw a freehand map of their neighborhood, visualizing what they see within a one-mile radius of their home and labeling places they consider most significant.

Student Artifact

Figure 2.1

A bulletin board display, like the one depicted in Figure 2.1, can create a community artifact from this assignment. Individually, students draw their maps for our classroom display, a bulletin board of individual student maps under the heading "I Belong to This Place." This heading reflects both individual and collective meanings. All students present the individual neighborhoods to which they belong, but the message and the display of each piece of student work send a constant reminder throughout the semester that each student belongs in the classroom space and, conversely, that the classroom belongs to them. This activity is one way to turn the classroom space into a community.

Teacher Reflection

Responses to this activity vary, but I have noticed that three distinct patterns emerge. Students who have just moved to the community tend to draw maps that reflect the cities they have left. The maps usually show outlines of a city as a whole rather than the details of just one neighborhood. The other two types of maps are either detailed sketches of the student's neighborhood that include his or her home, street names, and neighbors' houses with comments, or a simpler drawing with just three to four images (my house, my church, my school, etc.).

Students love to stand at the bulletin board and read one another's maps. They enjoy not only teasing one another about their artistic talents, but also trying to make a connection between the maps and their personal place in them. Comments include, "Oh, look, I live right around the corner from this map, Ms. Walker," and "Did Ryan draw this map? He is so cute! Look Chelsea, it's Ryan's house!" Sometimes the bulletin board serves as a meeting place. When students from other classes drop by to visit a friend, conversations are generated as they stand in front of the board and point to pictures, joke, and talk.

The year I initiated this lesson, I left the bulletin board up for almost the entire semester. When I finally replaced it because I wanted to display student illustrations from a novel we were reading, I was especially reluctant to take down the title "I Belong to This Place." I was so proud of this activity, and I felt it had become the theme of my classroom. But I did take it down because I sensed that we had become our own community and didn't need the sign anymore. New friendships had been formed, respect for the physical room and those who inhabited it had been exhibited, and a sense of ownership hung in the air.

This activity has become the way I start my class each new term. I break up the reading of the text into two days of forty-five-minute sessions. Reading for the entire ninety minutes of class is too much for both my tenth graders and me. Then they draw their maps. This activity can be completed in one class period, but I let them take home their maps to complete if they want.

This is a good way to start the school year. By the end of the third day of class, my students have read a novel, they have shared their place with their classmates, and they have begun creating a new, shared community.

Community ✛ Crossings

Suggestions on how you might adapt this lesson for a different classroom setting

- Older students could examine their school community by interviewing staff, students, and teachers. For younger students, various staff members (e.g., janitors, cafeteria workers, other teachers) could visit the class and discuss "their" school. As an extension, the students could write short narratives about their school and then create a quilt of their school's many communities (see Mimi Dyer's "Quilting Our Communities" in the Classroom Resources, Intermediate Lessons, on the KCAC Web site at http://kcac.kennesaw.edu/).

- Alternatively, students could ask people to map the school and how they experience it on a typical day. The maps could provide a springboard for discussion of how community members see the same place in different ways.

- Younger students could discuss with their parents where they were born and identify key historical aspects of the area. Students could then write poems that reflect their own birthplace and its historical significance. As an extension, parents could be invited to attend a reading of student poems.

- Students could use primary documents (e.g., land records, photographs, newspapers) to research the history of the land on which the school exists.

- For more established schools, students could compile a history of the institution, including major milestones and structural changes. Alternatively, students could establish an archive of the school, collecting primary documents that illuminate the school's history. Students could do oral histories with former students, teachers, and administrators (see Peggy Corbett's Hickory Flat Oral History Project, Chapter 10).

- Students could outline how their school fits within the larger community by developing a cluster map of community relationships.

- Because *My Place* tells the story of one locale through the eyes of the child narrators who inhabit that place in different time periods, the text is an excellent way to enliven and personalize the study of world history. For a fuller discussion of how to incorporate *My Place* into a history classroom, see Ed Hullender's "Re-Covering Imperial History" in the Extended Lesson Treatments section of Classroom Resources on the KCAC Web site at http://kcac.kennesaw.edu/.

II Single-Class-Period Activities

3 Take Two: Reading Community Photos

Mimi Dyer
Kennesaw Mountain High School, Marietta, Georgia

Overview

The primary guiding principle for this lesson is for students to develop a keen awareness of their community. I attempted to achieve this goal by having my students—in this case, AP language/composition seniors—do a close "reading" of photographs. My sense was that students might develop a deeper understanding of their community by viewing it through a different lens. I first discussed with them the origin of the word *community*; then I asked them to create a dictionary entry for the word. The KCAC project stresses that local communities continually redefine

School: Kennesaw Mountain High School
City: Marietta, Georgia
Grade level: 12
Discipline: Advanced Placement language and composition
School setting: suburban
Number of students: 11
Students in school: 2,000

themselves through material culture such as buildings, neighborhoods, parks, and public places, and that it is through study of this culture that we and our students can truly appreciate the essence of a community.

Shifting Landscapes,
Converging Peoples

Therefore, I purposely took pictures of Marietta, Georgia, that reflect change and difference in order to underscore the evolution of a community from a homogeneous, rural town to an international suburb dominated by housing developments and retail stores. These students were in the beginning stages of community-based research, so this exercise reinforced issues inherent in that process.

Students learn to become critical thinkers by engaging in activities that are relevant to their lives; in this case, I asked them to deconstruct their own backyards. And because they were familiar with many of the photographic sites, they had a better grasp of the lesson.

Another objective was to encourage discussion about how we choose photographic subjects. In other words, do we, or should we, have an agenda in the subjects we select for others to study? And if we do, is that okay? This part of the discussion fostered critical thinking and encouraged students to research cultures that have been left out of prior records of common life. Also, these texts reflected both the dynamic quality of local communities and the values that allow and encourage communities to keep or create certain representations.

Instructional Sequence

I took photos of community scenes suitable for my intended theme—in this case, the many faces of Marietta, Georgia—and had two prints made of each photo. The photos (see p. 17) included the following:

a. An Asian grocery store and gift shop, with signs in two languages

b. A strip mall with both English and Latino storefronts

c. A turn-of-the-century one-story barn

d. A sign announcing "A New American Town"—a planned community—established at the expense of beautiful forested land

e. A sign signaling the "Future Site of East Cobb Park" funded by private donations to preserve green space

f. A grocery display of eight different kinds of peppers

I talked the group through the sequence of events for the exercise so that they were aware of the entire process. This understanding helps students be comfortable with both the writing and the subsequent discussion.

I then distributed the pairs of photos to people not physically proximate to each other and asked them to freewrite for ten minutes about what in the image they see, don't see, feel, question, challenge, and so forth. This might be a good way to pair students who don't normally work together or students of different abilities. This approach affirms another principle integral to the KCAC project: that writing is crucial to developing communities of critical thinkers.

Participants then found the person with the same photo and shared their writing. They discussed similarities, differences, common threads, or other issues for about ten minutes.

Each pair shared the conclusions with the whole group, and the class was encouraged to offer further comments and questions. We spent the last few minutes analyzing the exercise, identifying the major lessons learned and suggesting ways to improve the activity.

Artifacts

Six pairs of photos (in this case, we had twelve participants, including me).

Student Reflections

Most of the students in this class were lifelong residents of Marietta, as were their parents before them, yet they were keenly aware of the changing demographics. One young man, however, was a first-generation immigrant from Cuba whose parents had sent him to live with relatives so that he could escape poverty and persecution. Throughout the semester, he had written about learning to speak English, growing up in a different culture, and finding his way as a young adult. During this particular class session, however, he remained on the outskirts, listening carefully to the swirling conversation about the changing community. Later he reflected that he thought of his classmates as the old Marietta, while he embodied the new. After a while, everyone noticed that he was not participating as energetically as he usually did; that's when they all gathered around, reassuring him that he too was part of the "new-new" community. For me this was a defining moment, for I realized then that the lesson had indeed taken root.

Student Conclusions about the Lesson

> The activity demonstrated the recent change in our community. Many of the pictures symbolized growth in population as well as diversity. The American Dream of freedom and prosperity now includes a widened Hispanic and Asian population.
>
> —Christen

> Our community has become a lot more diversified. We have cultural artifacts that range from Korean restaurants to wealthy townhomes.
>
> —Jennifer

> The community that we live in is changing. While the place where we live becomes more and more diverse, people never forget their pursuit of the American Dream.
>
> —Hollie

> Our community is comprised of a diverse demographic makeup that noticeably contrasts the historical demographics of the area. Certain traces of our interesting history as a rural farm area remain as old buildings symbolic of Cobb [County]'s past.
>
> —Justin

> Our community is not bound within the restrictions of one cultural group. Marietta is composed of myriad groups of cultures ranging from Oriental to Hispanic. That is a drastic difference to the predominantly white culture that was once Marietta.
>
> —Phil

> Our local community is culturally and monetarily diverse. It could be easy to pass our differences by, but with a closer inspection everything becomes clear.
>
> —Eric

> Many different cultures as well as historical elements combine to form the community in which we live.
>
> —Laura

Teacher Reflection

I chose this lesson as a result of the KCAC community's collective inquiry about how to use photographs effectively in the classroom, and I have implemented it several times, first with KCAC participants during the summer institute and then during a fall continuity night of the larger Kennesaw Mountain Writing Project community. Both groups of adults were on task throughout the exercise, and the lively discussions hit on the main themes of our project, yet the writing was descriptive and centered on broad generalities related to the idea of community. During the third iteration of the lesson, my students (the subjects of this chapter), perhaps because they were native to Marietta, and perhaps because we had developed a classroom community of our own, recognized the sites and were able to discuss in more depth the specific changes that had occurred and what those changes meant for our town. Most of their writing was analytical rather than descriptive, and all pairs questioned the implications for change that the images raised. Likewise, they were very aware of the editorial license I had taken in selecting the subjects, because they immediately commented on the fact that none of the photos was a coincidence for the purpose of the exercise. With this heightened awareness, they embraced thoughtful deconstruction and commentary even more heartily than their adult counterparts.

Finally, I used this lesson in a presentation to the 2002 National Writing Project Convention in Atlanta. In that venue, my audience hailed from all across the United States, and their energy was palpable. As a matter of fact, my portion of the session ran longer than expected because participants wanted to share their stories in response to the images. Their writing reflected their own places, from California to Florida, Michigan to Arizona, yet all understood the essence of change as it related to their own corners of the world. We heard tales of family, friends, landscapes, and histories, yet the voices sang the common song of reverence for culture even in the midst of change. The accents of our voices may have been different, but we sang the same refrain: we will continue to redefine ourselves as communities and discover that what divides us can also bind us together.

Community ✜ Crossings

Reflections on this lesson from Nebraska teacher Sharon Bishop

- Wright Morris, a Nebraska author and photographer, used black-and-white photographs "to celebrate the eloquence of structures so plainly dedicated to human use." Morris's photos rarely depict people; instead, he wants the viewer to project his or her own story into the picture. He was fond of using as his subjects items that showed they had been worn out from the inside out. Since Morris's writing is too difficult for many students to read, a study of his photography introduces students to this author. Asking students to photograph a place in the style of Morris pushes them to look at the region with different eyes. Morris was not interested in a "dressed-up" version, something students typically produce, especially when using color film. But the black-and-white photographs students have taken have been stunning. Morris combined his pictures with equally austere narrative prose to create what many critics have hailed as a new art form. Many of my students have taken my assignment to a higher level by composing words *and* photos.

- Since Nebraska is a rural, agricultural area, many students engaged in this activity will show how farms and farm machinery have changed over the years. Since the area is not culturally diverse, most communities don't change much; however, if students visit other towns in the area, which is easy for them to do, they will immediately see that the main streets of many small towns in Nebraska now reflect Latino influences. A study of historical photos of community businesses will show students how small towns have been altered by changes in communication and transportation.

- This assignment also allows students to discover for themselves that knowledge of one's place includes the concept of change. This could also allow students to predict what a place will look like in twenty-five years. Will there even be small rural towns? Who will live in them? What businesses might be in them? Will there be a school—will future school consolidations continue? What will farms be like? What will the land look like? When students interview elders about the changes in a community, when they study the ways a place has changed in one or two generations, they not only are better critical thinkers, but they can also imagine themselves as agents of change rather than powerless in the face of those inevitable changes.

4 Viewfinders: Students Picturing Their Communities

Gerri Hajduk
Wheeler High School, Marietta, Georgia

Overview

Photographs play an important role in the overall memory of families, of communities, and of a particular time in history. Using photography enables students to study the past and present conditions of the communities in which they live and become knowledgeable and involved citizens. Students usually enjoy taking photographs, and this can be an exciting way to help students learn about history and their community through a different lens.

> **School:** Wheeler High School
> **City:** Marietta, Georgia
> **Grade level:** 11
> **Discipline:** Advanced Placement
>   U.S. history
> **School setting:** suburban to urban
> **Number of students:** 56
> **Students in school:** 1,700

Instructional Sequence

This introductory activity prepares students for an assignment that includes work outside of class.

1. The teacher prepares students by discussing the importance of photography in U.S. history from the time of the Civil War to the present. The class studies and discusses several photos from different historic periods.

Shifting Landscapes, Converging Peoples

Building Cities

2. To help students learn the process of "reading" a photograph, the teacher leads the students through two activities using selected photos:

a. The teacher will have prepared a set of photos (two of each subject) of the community. Each student writes a reaction to one photo. This is a good time to ask the students to look for what is *not* in the picture that might be of importance. Photo partners (those who have identical photos) then come together to discuss how each reacted to the photograph. Reactions should then be shared with the entire class.

b. The teacher provides each student with a historically significant photograph. The image might be of a local scene, but it could also reference national or international events. The goal, in any case, is to develop a critical eye. First, the student is asked to write down his or her overall impression of the photo. The student is then asked to divide the picture into quadrants, look more closely at each section, and list three things that might be inferred from the photograph as a whole. This should raise some questions and encourage students to do a much closer reading of the photograph.

3. In class, discuss some of the tensions, changes, historic sites, or icons in the community. The depth of the discussion will depend on the particular class and how much information the teacher wants to give the students as a lead-in to the extended assignment that follows.

a. The students are then instructed to take pictures of several sites that depict change, tension, historic significance, or community icons.

b. After careful consideration, the student then chooses one photograph that best exemplifies the topic. The student mounts the photo, writes an appropriate caption, and writes a brief explanation of what the photo portrays and why he or she chose that particular image.

c. Each student then shares with the class the photograph and observations.

Student Artifacts

"Typical Suburbia"—This picture [Figure 4.1] says it all. A red minivan with a soccer ball magnet parked by the Gap at the Avenue. In the area we live in, this is the typical car. This is the typical suburban scene. All day Saturday, Mom and Dad sit in the folding chairs at Metro North Soccer Fields watching Mom Jr. and Dad Jr. run all over the field, not really knowing in which direction to run. It doesn't matter what happens; if Mom Jr. or Dad Jr. even touches the ball, Mom and Dad go nuts. Can you believe it? That's my girl (or boy)! Sunday mornings are spent at Johnson Ferry Baptist Church. Afterwards, the family goes to J. Christopher's for brunch. Later, Dad Jr. goes outside and tosses the baseball with Dad, while Mom Jr., glove on hand, tries to keep up. Mom is watching from the window as she peels potatoes. Isn't life grand? On Monday, Mom wakes up and sees Dad off. She then wakes up Mom Jr. and Dad Jr. and puts two slices of toast in the toaster. Mom Jr. and Dad Jr. rush downstairs, so as not to miss the bus. A quick kiss on Mom's cheek, and both kids are out of the door, brown lunchbags in hand. After making herself a cup of tea, watching Katie Couric on

Figure 4.1

the *Today* show, popping a load in the laundry, showering, and making herself up, Mom decides to pick up some groceries for dinner tonight. Afterwards, she decides to stop at Borders and buy *Heart of a Woman*, the Kathie Lee CD. While at Borders, she walks down to the Gap to see if they have any cute little outfits for Mom Jr. That brings us up to this point.

Seriously, though—this picture completely captures the very essence of life in East Cobb, your typical suburb. The Mom drives the minivan with the soccer ball sticker. Dad drives the Lexus or BMW. In a few years, they will buy a Jeep for Dad Jr., and he will put a Walton [High School] license plate on the front. And this is how life goes for so many American families living in suburbia ALL OVER. It's the same story everywhere. This is not a cynical view. Of course, there are small differences, and families cannot be duplicated across the board, but this is just a typical scene in a typical parking lot in a typical suburb.

—Bennett

Figure 4.2

"Winecoff"—This photograph [Figure 4.2] juxtaposes multiple aspects of Atlanta. Taken on Peachtree Street, it contrasts the old Atlanta landmarks with the new. In the foreground, a tapestry celebrating the Martin Luther King Jr. parade hangs from a lamppost installed and dedicated during the Olympics. The sign, the clock, whose time has long since stopped, and the awning of the oldest department store in Georgia remember a time when King walked its streets. The gray and white brick of the Winecoff hotel bears witness to the greatest hotel fire in history. Next to it, a plaque tells the story of the luxurious Ritz Carlton located just across the street. One Atlanta street corner tells of decades of Southern living.

—Ben

Teacher Reflection

The extended project that grew from the single-class discussion activity described at the start of this chapter turned out to be a great success. Both the students and their parents enjoyed it, and it forced the students to think about what was important enough to photograph and share with their peers. Making photo selections to represent their ideas about a community space promoted critical-thinking skills.

The images students chose varied from plaques about Leo Frank (a Jewish man lynched in Marietta in 1915), Turner Field (where the Atlanta Braves play), and the Big Chicken (a local landmark restaurant), to a homeless man getting a haircut (in downtown Atlanta). In fact, I was pleased to see how many of my suburban students chose to take pictures in downtown Atlanta, indicating that they see themselves as active members of the larger metropolitan community. The photographs were displayed at Open House, and the parents were vocal in their enthusiasm for the assignment, especially because it required students to be decision makers. One parent who had accompanied his son into downtown Atlanta to take photos was excited to see that decision-making process in action—e.g., picking scenes, setting up camera angles, and considering the "meaning" of particular social spaces. Many of the photographs from that first year were selected for the school literary magazine.

After my first experience with this assignment, I decided to expand the requirements. Beginning in the second year, I asked students to create a collage rather than a single image. Students selected a unifying theme about community life and then took photographs related to their topic. One major requirement of the new assignment was to arrange the photos on a display board in a way that would tell a story about their theme. Topics have included the role of churches in one small suburban community; varying approaches for representing patriotism (e.g., flags, signs); cross-race relations within the high school population; "Shades of Green" (i.e., the use of green spaces) in the suburbs; and selection of names for streets in our community. Besides preparing their collage, students write captions for each picture and an extended reflection in which they describe their process for preparing the display—everything from choosing their topic to finding locations to photograph, arranging their images, and preparing their oral presentations to the whole class.

This expanded version of the assignment taps into students' critical-thinking skills even more than the first approach. Students are able to select their own specific topics from a broad list of issues (diversity, problems facing the community, local heritage, and social interactions). Thus, one student examined diversity by gathering images from a range of new commercial sites in the area (e.g., a barber shop, a car dealership, restaurants, and a branch bank, some of which are using Spanish-language signs now), whereas another recorded scenes at a local elementary school. One student questioned the impact of construction projects on our school's neighborhood by creating a before-and-after record of clear-cutting trees to build new subdivisions, whereas another looked photographically at varying styles of architecture being used in new housing developments. Having to choose, research, and represent findings for a specific theme connected to one of the larger issues about contemporary life that we are exploring as a class promotes more in-depth products than those produced in the first version of this project.

In American Studies classrooms like mine, this project has been especially effective for connecting the study of history with writing, presentation skills, and cultural analysis. Taking and displaying their own photographs helps students develop aesthetic sensibilities, but it also enhances their ability to interpret illustrations, historical images (e.g., the famous painting of Washington crossing the Delaware), and photo-journalism's historical texts (such as Civil War and Gilded Age photography). When students take the AP history test at the end of the year and find illustrations in the document-based question, they are well prepared to analyze those texts.

When we gather all the displays together in the classroom, we build a sense of our own community. Not only have we looked at particular aspects of the community individually but, with the assembled displays brought together, we also acquire a more complete picture of where we live than any single product could promote on its own. This sharing time, which is central to the project, also helps students see how academic research is a cumulative, ongoing process of knowledge building with public significance.

Now, every year when students begin my American Studies course, they ask, "When do we get to do the photo project?" This assignment has become such a well-known highlight of our program that students begin the course already thinking about how they will tackle the project.

Community ✧ Crossings

Suggestions on how you might adapt this lesson for a different classroom setting

- Students might photograph before-and-after scenes in rural, urban, or suburban America—the land or buildings before destruction or renovation and the structures or reconfigurations afterward. This juxtaposition might work well to bookend the semester, allowing students to note patterns of change over time where they live.

- Provide students with historical photographs of their community and ask them to locate and rephotograph these areas to begin a historical examination of place.

- An environmental science class could photograph suburban developments, landmarks, and activities to prompt a visual analysis of community change as defined by that discipline.

5 Giving Students a Penny for Their Thoughts

Oreather J. Bostick-Morgan, T. H. Slater School, Atlanta

Overview

My affiliation with the Keeping and Creating American Communities project (especially with colleagues exploring the Shifting Landscapes, Converging Peoples theme) led me to collaborate with other teachers in my building who shared an interest in documenting some of the changes occurring in our community. Our primary goal was to generate student interest in the project while integrating curricular objectives that were to be covered during the school year. My agenda was a little more involved than theirs because of my focus. I wanted to make certain that I followed the

School: T. H. Slater School
City: Atlanta
Grade level: K–5
Discipline: speech-language (multidisciplinary studies)
School setting: urban
Number of students: 28
Students in school: 360

guiding principles supported by both the National Writing Project and the KCAC collaborative.

Selected teachers from my building and I met to discuss the plan for implementing our project. My specific focus was to provide a language experience approach that would elicit inquisitive behaviors from my students, an approach based on the research of Ashton-Warner and

Building Cities

of Stauffer. When teachers help students to connect their reading and thinking processes to the world around them, especially their local communities, students become active and interested readers. This relationship has been validated again and again through research and continues to prove successful as a literacy strategy. I also wanted to support the core practices of the NWP by providing opportunities for collaboration that would foster the "teacher teaching teachers" model and build a classroom community respectful of the diversity each person brings, one that embraces higher-level cognitive skills by engaging students in analyzing and critiquing the artifacts they obtain and the stories they experience.

We decided to include in our lesson plans the standards we could address across the curriculum as consistent with students' individualized goals and objectives. The high degree of correlation between state standards and KCAC principles suggests that community-building curricular initiatives are not antithetical to standards-based initiatives. Teachers can pursue both state standards and community inquiry. In so doing, teachers can provide students with rigorous yet relevant classroom experiences.

Objectives

1. Defining ourselves, who we are, and our sense of place.
2. Obtaining historical information about the area of Atlanta where our school is located.
3. Identifying changes of the past and the present

Instructional Sequence

Like some other single-session lessons described in this section of the book, the following learning activity became a springboard to a multiday sequence of activities. In this case, after a few minutes of teacher modeling on one day, students spent the following class period writing about the year of their birth. Later, follow-up activities, inspired by the success of the first lesson, extended the approach so that students ultimately created their own *All about Me* penny books.

The teacher begins this activity by having the class read *Aunt Flossie's Hats* by Elizabeth Fitzgerald Howard and then discuss how this is a book of memories. We all have memories we can share if we choose, and a good way to remember some of these memories is to concentrate on a specific time. The teacher selects a penny dated the year something special happened to him or her and models making a rubbing of the penny on a flip chart and writing about that experience. Students are given an assignment to bring a penny to school dated the year they were born. They also interview parents, grandparents, guardians, or caregivers to gather data about that early period in their lives.

Before the students start writing, the teacher guides whole-group discussions about their interviews to generate definitions for unfamiliar words and phrases that may need to be added to word study lists or word walls. (I found that as students discussed their interviews, they clarified and organized their ideas, used more specific vocabulary, and extended their understanding of what actually happened. Those students who did not previously recall their date of birth also left the experience conversant about the date, time, and place of their birth.)

Possible extensions of this activity: Students might include artifacts or popular music from their year of birth; research what was going on in the world at that time; draw illustrations to accompany the text; and then revise, edit, and share their findings in writer's workshop. They might then add these items to their portfolio for publication. The teacher might also encourage students to make connections from the past to the present through comparing and contrasting the two periods. It is best if the comparison rests on something concrete that can be contrasted both verbally (in writing) and visually (in images such as photography or illustration). The following artifact demonstrates how students can use classroom technology (here, Microsoft PowerPoint) to combine visual and verbal texts in order to compare the past to the present. The key to making this artifact successful was the concrete item—the trash can—that served as the springboard for student reflection and writing.

Student Artifact

See excerpts from "The Way It Was in Our Grandmother's Backyard," a PowerPoint presentation by Ahmaud and Rashad, in Figure 5.1.

Teacher Reflection

I will long remember this initiative as pivotal to the way I now teach language. Combining history, social studies, language (oral and written), math, and other disciplines inspired in my students a true appreciation for their own histories. Initially, I began with the idea that I would be sharing with and facilitating for my students, but I ended up having an experience with my students very different from the one I had anticipated. Ultimately, my students taught me to value their history.

I had long been comfortable teaching speech and language processes through the use of personal histories, but with this assignment I decided to add options for publication. I had previously used portions of this lesson with some of my students but had never considered offering their personal histories for publication outside of our classroom. The students always became motivated to write based on their personal experiences, so I decided to use the pennies of history as a launching pad to incite a desire for writing throughout the year.

The Way It Was In Our Grandmother's Backyard

By Ahmaud and Rashad Blake

Peer Edited and Published by: The Speech Lady,
Mrs. Bostick-Morgan

The Way Trashcans Were

- We found in the ground trashcans.
- We use to have trash cans in the ground. The trash cans in the ground were made of metal. The liners in the trash cans were made of metal. Rashad almost fell in. It was filled up with leaves and other dirty stuff.

The Way It Is Now

- Now we have trash cans in the kitchen. Now the trash cans in the kitchen are made of plastic. The liners for our trashcans are plastic bags.
- Amaud and I have to take out the trash and put it in a bigger trashcan that we push down to the street.

Figure 5.1

Sharing penny-based writing on different years became a regular classroom practice, helping students gradually build a collection of personal writing tied to various years of their lives. We read and discussed a variety of books written in different genres and discussed ways of integrating technology into our efforts. As my students learned about memoir, those same students who often said "I don't know anything to write about" had so much to share each time I pulled out my penny jar. I asked the students to select a penny, figure out how old they were in that year, think of a WOW! experience to share, and write about it. The products we completed as a part of this initiative were wonderful to behold, but I had not considered that in teaching this way I might cause students to share pieces of themselves they would not want to share with the world. Choosing an arbitrary year elicits both positive and negative life experiences, and my students wrote about both types *for themselves.* When I encouraged them to share these pieces with a broader audience, many of them, Ahmaud and Rashad included, were reluctant to publish the pieces they valued the most because the experiences were private memories of difficult times. Because they learned to value these pieces of their own histories, we were limited in selections we could agree to publish. Finally we agreed on one memoir to include from this process. The memoir Ahmaud and Rashad selected was one they shared happily because it did not speak to their trials or even to their triumphs. The piece here is impersonal and safer than some of the more powerful and effective pieces my students wrote.

Even though I wasn't able to include these more powerful and personal pieces in this book, I'm glad that I gave my students the opportunity to write them. I was humbled as I saw students later collecting pictures of experiences from summer vacations, mentoring, and other opportunities to add to their growing journal about themselves. The impact had been profound on both me and my students.

Many of the lessons the students taught me were familiar but were revalidated in this journey:

- My students become truly motivated when they see how much I value their lived experiences.
- Students need lots of time to reflect, write, revise, and edit. Nothing beats allowing students the time to work on one piece of writing until they are satisfied with it.
- Teachers can cover a multitude of objectives in one activity.
- Spelling and vocabulary can grow by leaps and bounds, even for students with learning disabilities, when they are provided "mouth time" to use new vocabulary in conversation.

- Making students responsible for their own learning, giving them choices, supporting them when they reach an impasse, and encouraging the small gains boost self-esteem and motivate learning.

This activity was a great experience for all of us. I now use portions of the introductory penny lesson as an icebreaker for students to share bits of themselves at the beginning of school. This oral activity supports students as they develop their oral language skills. It also allows me to listen for the way they organize their thoughts and helps me better plan how to provide them with other opportunities that will motivate them to stick with an assigned task even if they think it is too difficult.

Community ✜ Crossings

Suggestions on how you might adapt this lesson for a different classroom setting

- This activity is an effective way to help young people move into the research process in a less threatening way than traditional research assignments. Another benefit is that it removes the possibility of receiving the "encyclopedia" paper that all teachers dread. As students interview family members about the date on their pennies, they are actively involved in using primary sources and legitimately gathering data. The activity provides opportunities to develop listening, reading, and writing skills in a meaningful context. And what subject could be more interesting to a child than his or her own childhood?

- Beginning with a penny to research a date provides students with an object lesson in identifying a concrete artifact that connects to abstract, historical concepts. This piece of copper begins the brainstorming process of recalling or exploring events or cultural shifts that occurred within that year: political, environmental, sociological, economic, scientific, familial, and more. Although the activity was implemented in a third-grade classroom, higher elementary, middle school, and high school teachers might also find this approach valuable.

- The penny provides a way for students to research their personal histories, but it could also be used to encourage students to examine historical trends within that year. Likewise, researching all the complex forces that combine to create a penny would be useful. The symbols selected to appear on the penny to illustrate American values are worth examining. How does the U.S. Treasury work? Why might the penny become obsolete? What economic lessons might be learned? How might it be compared to currency in other countries?

How do coins illustrate the values and beliefs of a country? The ideas derived from this single coin could stimulate multiple complex research and critical-thinking activities.

- A by-product of this exercise is that students begin to see themselves against a backdrop that has a much broader scope than just their neighborhood. As they discuss events surrounding their births, they are able to see that they are part of this thing called history, which they sometimes think exists only in history books. With the use of the Internet, students could further research historic events; the activity has great collaborative potential because students in the class would share birth years within probably a three-year period.

6 A Correspondence between Atlanta Students

Dave Winter
Henry W. Grady High School, Atlanta

Overview

I knew that once we started engaging our communities that we would all become history teachers. You can't very well explore past heritages situated within a particular place and not become in some sense a teacher of history. What I didn't know is how changing teaching jobs would literally transform my professional space from an honors American literature classroom in suburban Atlanta to an Advanced Placement U.S. history classroom in Midtown.

> **School:** Henry W. Grady High School
> **City:** Atlanta
> **Grade level:** 11
> **Discipline:** Advanced Placement U.S. history
> **School setting:** urban
> **Number of students:** 45
> **Students in school:** 900

The distinction between the history classroom and the literature classroom had become blurred in the courses of many of my KCAC colleagues. Their work shows how students can use the methods of a historian to recover the narratives of their own lives. The same is true of the history of one's community. When Peggy Corbett and her advanced English students embarked on a mission to recover and rescue the heritage of Hickory Flat in rural Cherokee County, her students became true historians. Even more important, they not only made history, but they also put that history to use in pursuing a noble goal in the present.

Educating for Citizenship

But there are two kinds of history. One kind, the primary kind that community studies work represents, involves recovery through documenting the past. The other kind, the secondary kind evaluated by state and national history standards and monolithic tests like the College

Board's Advanced Placement test, requires that students master information that has already been recovered, verified, and institutionalized in the secondary curriculum. Creating primary history is more engaging than learning secondary history, but the two objectives compete for finite classroom time.

The great thing about this project (and, dare I say, this book) is that you don't have to devote an entire semester or even an entire unit to this approach to bring it into your classroom. So I thought smaller. Benefiting from the wonderful recovery work of my colleagues in the Educating for Citizenship strand of KCAC (especially Deborah Mitchell and Ed Hullender) and the generosity of Taronda Spencer, the archivist at Spelman College, I devised the two-hour lesson that follows. It's based on a newspaper column written in 1886 by a Spelman senior, Carrie P. Walls. The column, addressed as an open letter to "My Dear Little Folks of the North and South" (included in full in this chapter), recounts Ms. Walls's teaching experience in a small Georgia community. Rich in specific historical detail, the letter also provides insight into Ms. Walls's perspective and her motivation in relating her experience to the multiple audiences to which she was writing.

The document provides a firsthand look at the partially Reconstructed South, one that is very different from the sweeping textbook accounts of radicals, scalawags, carpetbaggers, and Booker T. Washington. By providing a set of analytical focus questions to guide their reading and by giving them a range of response-writing opportunities, I hoped to encourage my students to interrogate both the primary document and the secondary accounts found in their textbook.

Instructional Sequence

This exercise in critical reading and writing achieves two objectives: (1) it encourages students to see history from multiple perspectives, especially in voices underrepresented in their survey textbook, and (2) it encourages them to interrogate assumptions and biases that shape the presentation of history in their survey text.

Materials: Pen and paper or computer time. Copies of the primary document, in this case Carrie P. Walls's November 1886 letter, which appeared in *The Spelman Messenger* under the column heading "Children's Exchange."

Time: Approximately two hours over two days.

1. Students should have read and/or discussed the textbook presentation of Reconstruction and post–Reconstruction schooling before beginning this activity.

2. Distribute the copies of the letter and have the students read it. You can also distribute the guided reading questions or, if you prefer, hold the questions and use them to direct an open discussion.

Questions for student response or for discussion:

a. What facts about Ms. Walls can we determine for certain from the letter? What can we infer about her from context?

b. What is the main message of the letter? What specific information does she convey? Is she attempting to inform, to persuade, to amuse, to inspire, or something else entirely?

c. To whom is Ms. Walls writing? What is (are) her primary audience (or audiences)?

d. In what ways does this letter reinforce or complement the presentation of this historical period in the textbook?

e. In what ways does it depart from or contradict the textbook presentation? How do you account for this disparity?

f. What broader conclusion about history can you draw from the comparison of these documents? What role must the historian play in creating both primary and secondary sources? Which is more reliable? Which is more influential?

g. Write a definition of history that includes how historians and students of history should deal with primary and secondary documents.

3. The teacher guides class discussion that more fully fleshes out the answers to these questions.

4. Students complete a closure writing assignment.

Possibilities:

a. Creative

i. Write an imagined response to Ms. Walls in the voice of the "Little Folks of the North and South" to whom she is writing.

ii. Imagine that Ms. Walls has assigned her students the task of writing to the same audience to which she wrote her column. Write the imagined letter in the voice of Ms. Walls's star student.

iii. Write an imagined letter to the editor of *The Spelman Messenger* from a Northern philanthropist articulating how he feels about his continued support of Spelman and explaining why he will or will not continue to support the school financially.

    b. Analytical

        i. Much of the message of Ms. Walls's letter is implied. Contrast the literal message of the letter with its implied message.

        ii. Discuss how Ms. Walls's letter and her experience complicate the textbook discussion of the post–Reconstruction South.

        iii. Discuss the role of the historian in presenting the history of disadvantaged peoples as both victims of discrimination and agents combating it. How does the historian balance issues of representation against issues of accuracy and significance?

    c. Speculative

        i. Explore the possible uses a historian might have for this letter and the other archives stored and largely uncategorized at Spelman and elsewhere. Relate this reflection to the definition of history you wrote earlier.

        ii. What is more significant in history: information or narrative? How does your answer affect the relative significance of Ms. Walls's letter?

Evaluation: Evaluating this activity might be as simple as direct questioning of each student during discussion. The teacher might assess the student writing formally, either holistically or more rigorously with a content expectation for each question or essay prompt.

Necessary Handout

Carrie P. Walls, "Children's Exchange," *Spelman Messenger* (November 1886): 6.

> My Dear Little Folks of the North and South:
>
> I think you will like to hear about the summer school of a Spelman girl, and I always like to please the little folks. My school was in Rock Fence, one hundred and forty-two miles east from Atlanta, and fourteen miles in the country from Elberton, the shiretown of the county. I have taught there two terms. My schoolhouse, a rude log hut, fifteen by ten, also serves as the church of the district. It stands in a beautiful pine grove and has a very large pleasant playground. The school this year numbering forty-two, thirty of them being boys. The reason there are so few girls is, many of the parents think it useless to educate their daughters so do not send them. I opened school every morning at eight o'clock with the Lord's Prayer which the pupils repeated after me. In this way many of them learned it. We next repeated a passage of Scripture

in the same way, after which I explained it as well as I could. This exercise was followed by singing; then came the recitations which continued until five o'clock in the afternoon.

While teaching in those log huts we were very much troubled when the summer storms came up, because when the rain poured, we could scarcely find a dry place in the house; but if the wind came with the rain we were much worse off. When it blew from the south I crowded my scholars into the north side of the room; if from the north, we went to the south side; thus we traveled till the rain was over. Sometimes the rain seemed to come in on all sides, then I raised my umbrella and did the best I could. In spite of these things I enjoyed teaching, and felt that I might be worse off, for one of the neighboring teachers had to raise his umbrella on clear days to protect him from the sun which poured its burning rays through the open roof.

During our vacation, when we are away from our pleasant home (Spelman) we not only teach but try to live by the text, "Freely ye have received, freely give." As our dear teachers give us from their store of knowledge so we try to give to those who have less advantages.

I hope the little friends who read this will all the more appreciate their pleasant homes and their opportunities for going to school, remembering that these children of who I have written are taught but three months in the year.

My home is in Columbus, Georgia. This is my fourth year in this school and Spelman is to me the happiest home in the South. I remain yours,

Cousin Carrie

Student Artifacts

The following are sample responses—written in class without revision—to the response topics included in the instructional sequence outlined earlier.

a. Creative
ii. Imagine that Ms. Walls has assigned her students the task of writing to the same audience to which she wrote her column. Write the imagined letter in the voice of Ms. Walls's star student.

Dear Ladies and Gentlemen of the North and South,

My name is Bernard Cookeman, and I am 16 years old. I'll be legal age in a year and half, but this is only my third term at school. I used to work in the summers on Mr. Simkins' farm to help my mama and papa. My daddy lost his leg in the war and I have four younger brothers and sisters. My mama works as a cook for Lady Daniels in town, so we ain't got much. I gave all the money I earned to my papa and he let me go to school in the summers.

I like going to school. My teacher Ms. Walls says I read real good. She gives me books to take home from time to time. My favorite story is "Rip Van Winkle." Sometimes I stay after school with Ms. Walls and she helps me read scriptures from the Bible. I'm good with numbers too. I memorized all my multiplication tables in two weeks. Ms. Walls says I'm her top pupil even though most of the other children have been going to school longer. Ms. Walls is really nice and all the children like her. Every morning we recite the Lord's Prayer and she reads to us during lunch. The first year I came to school my teacher was an old man named Professor Edwards. He was from Massachusetts and would whip the students when we couldn't recite our lessons.

I want to be just like Ms. Walls when I get older. I want to go to Morehouse College and become a minister. Ms. Walls says if I keep on reading and work hard on my numbers I can go to college like she did. In the summers I'll come back to Rock Fence and teach in the same log cabin to other pupils. I'll make them recite a prayer every morning just like Ms. Walls.

I know I'm lucky to go to school. None of my younger brothers and sisters knows how to read or count. My mama doesn't read well either. When I become a minister I'll teach all my brothers and sisters how to read and count to one hundred. I'll teach them to read scriptures and recite lessons, just like Ms. Walls taught me.

Sincerely,
Bernard Cookeman

—Morgan

b. Analytical
ii. Discuss how Ms. Walls's letter and her experience complicate the textbook discussion of the post–Reconstruction South.

Ms. Walls' letter and her experience complicate the textbook's discussion of the post-Reconstruction South. Ms. Walls' experience is not what most African-Americans experienced during that time. Many blacks did not have the opportunity to attend an institute of higher learning. Most blacks at the time, particularly in the post-Reconstruction South, had to find immediate means of survival. Blacks had to take to sharecropping or other means of survival. Many did not have the money to send their child to school or could not afford to lose their child's services at home.

Since what I just wrote is what actually was the situation in the South at that time, including Ms. Walls' experience complicates historical accounts in textbooks. First, history cannot include everyone's story. In history, one should discuss what occurred in most instances. That way, you learn about what most people during that time experienced. When you include Ms. Walls' experience, one in which only a handful of blacks had the opportunity to participate, you are giving a false account of what actually happened. You are twisting history into something that really had no significance. Ms. Walls' experience was a nice story but should be mentioned as an afterthought of the time, not the plight of blacks at the time.

—Chris

c. Speculative
ii. What is more significant in history: information or narrative? How does your answer affect the relative significance of Ms. Walls's letter?

Narratives written by historians, rather than a person who was involved in the event, present more of the information about and around the event than would those who had involvement. The event as interpreted by a participant will seem more exciting than the narrative by a historian because the person was actually involved, especially in cases of disaster. If a historian were to tell you about the Japanese attack on Pearl Harbor on Dec. 7, 1941, you would hear mainly about how we were surprised on a Sunday morning, how many ships and aircraft were destroyed at little cost to the enemy, and how "thankfully, our carriers were at sea and were not damaged, helping us to end the war in the Pacific more swiftly." Perhaps, somewhere in the middle of all the information, there might be a mention of the great loss of life that coincided with the loss of machinery. That would about cover the information side of the event. The narrative side, however, would draw more attention because it would be a human-interest story. If someone were to write a book, or broadcast their story of escape from the Battleship Arizona, the sinking of which occurred during this same event, the tales of flames and screaming, dying men, would attract more readers than a relation of numbers.

Though narratives are more entertaining, information is a very important part of history. Future generations of humans, as we have done, will look for the simplified versions of history, more often than not, how their home country, state, or region had an effect on history. Few people remember the triumph of Sgt. Alvin York during World War I, where he captured or killed (even I do not remember the number exactly but to the best of my ability) 200 German soldiers by himself. More recall that World War I ended in triumph for the Allies with the Treaty of Versailles. For the ease of quick accessibility in the mind, information is better: to remember things as a whole, rather than an individual's actions.

Both narratives and information are useful, but information is more useful when speaking of history. Narratives tend to engage the human aspect, where information regards whole events and is more easily remembered.

—Elliott

Teacher Reflection

My earlier work with the National Writing Project has convinced me that students need to *make* literature, not just *study* it. In the same way, my involvement with the KCAC project has led me to understand that my students also need to *make* history, not just *study* it.

Given the opportunity to analyze Carrie Walls's piece or to respond to it creatively, my students overwhelmingly chose the latter. That's hardly surprising, I guess, but it does serve as an important reminder that teachers should look for ways to encourage creativity in students' responses to primary documents. Teachers don't have to sacrifice analysis for creativity; in fact, they can get their students to analyze material more deeply through less traditional and more creative assessments. Many times the students perform the analysis without realizing they are doing it.

After the in-class writing of these responses, a few of the students asked to take home their pieces for revision, but most—including most of those printed here—wrote the piece wholly in class. Writing well and polishing can be important aspects of this process, but I think it's important for teachers to realize that students can write reflectively and informally as a way of thinking more clearly and analyzing more deeply. Teachers can meet this objective whether or not the students revise in pursuit of a polished piece of writing.

I was pleased when the activity provided two of the best, most animated discussions of the entire year, and I also found it interesting that the writers willing to delve into the analytical questions seemed more likely to dismiss the column's relevance, while those who valued it more opted to respond to the creative prompts. Chris, for example, was most consistent in his comments in class and on paper, but his adversaries in class discussion—who defended the merits of representation and agency just as forcefully as Chris downplayed them—chose to write creatively. In class, most of the students disagreed with Chris's dismissal. They pointed out that omitting attempts to combat inequities and discrimination (or viewing them as insignificant) would paint an inaccurate historical picture of this period. Multiple perspectives do more than honor a disadvantaged group; they provide a richer, more textured and truthful history.

But the arguments that surfaced in class did not always surface clearly on paper. I would conclude then that a student's choice to enter the historical moment (and write from it creatively) is in many ways a validation of the moment's significance.

I wish I had been able to discuss the students' written responses more with them, but the Panic of 1893 waits for no one. I did, however, note their heightened animation. Students' enthusiasm motivated me to find more ways to encourage their active engagement in primary sources closer to home the following year.

Community ✤ Crossings

Suggestions on how you might adapt this lesson for a different classroom setting

- This lesson's value extends to the use of many types of primary documents. Students can be given opportunities to analyze and draw inferences from information that emerges from traditional historical documents, including letters and diaries, and from more personal and immediate documents, such as yearbooks, architectural blueprints, and historical photographs.

- Improve student understanding of the historian's process of studying, analyzing, and evaluating the value of documents by examining a variety of primary documents. Discuss with students the idea that much of our knowledge of the past is determined through this type of analysis. The Library of Congress Web site (see the bibliography) provides a number of resources for this type of activity.

- Elementary students might examine copies of their parents' or other adults' yearbooks. What do the clothing, hairstyles, and background scenery reveal about the subjects and the setting? How does an examination of the subject in that setting inform the student?

- Newspaper articles, editorials, and letters provide an alternative representation of history. Secondary students might discuss the disparity between a textbook representation of a historical event and the public record of that event.

- Invite students to examine the setting of a work of fiction and to discuss how the historical backdrop of the plot controls the characters' actions, dialogue, decisions, and so on. Have students analyze whether the actions are consistent with the history of the setting.

- Students of all ages might use their baby books as a primary document. What is revealed about the child, parents, and/or family through what was chosen for inclusion in the baby book? Scrapbooks and photo albums offer additional resources for analysis.

III Units/Major Assignments

7 Setting the Stage for Historical Fiction

Bernadette Lambert, Cobb County Public Schools, Georgia

Overview

Visualizing is an excellent strategy to help students better understand a text, especially a historical work to which the students bring limited background knowledge. The following novel study of Joseph Bruchac's *The Journal of Jesse Smoke: A Cherokee Boy* merges the visualizing strategy with classroom theater applications from community and performance studies to produce an engaging vehicle for taking middle school students to a higher level of understanding about a specific moment in history.

> This novel study was done with eighteen eighth-grade students in a suburban public school with a diverse student body. The students involved were average readers in a homogeneous literacy class that met for thirty-five minutes daily. The novel we read was a Dear America series book, *The Journal of Jesse Smoke: A Cherokee Boy* by Joseph Bruchac.

Instructional Sequence

Considering the Importance of Historical Evidence

Before students received the novel or even knew its subject, we spent a class period thinking about different types of primary resources and how they could be used to create historical records.

Reclaiming Displaced Heritages

I distributed various items and instructed students to work in pairs to make inferences about the person who had owned the artifact. This led to a discussion of the importance of accurate and authentic artifacts for the sharing of historical information.

Activating and Building Background Knowledge

We spent a class period completing a history story frame for the Trail of Tears by drawing on the students' prior knowledge from their study of Georgia history. The history story frame considers the basic elements of a story: title, characters, setting, plot, resolution, and theme. We filled in what the students already knew about the Trail of Tears; then we read a short piece from a visitors' guide to the Cherokee Indian Reservation in North Carolina. Using their own familiarity with the topic and their reading of the visitors' guide, students quickly identified the key players, dates, places, basic time line, resolution, and even the beginnings of a theme, or "so what" statement, for the historical events we would be reading about in more detail in the novel. Taken together, this work built a strong foundation for the text before students had even begun reading the book.

Defining a Purpose to Read and Organizing for Reading and Discussion

After students surveyed the book, including a map and several photographs, I read aloud the first two diary entries. I then distributed reading logs in which I had divided the book into twelve sections to help with the pacing of the reading. I modeled my expectations for each section by explaining one significant scene that I would want to stage if I turned the book into a play. For the scene, I wrote the sequence of events, the characters involved, and one significant artifact that needed to be in the scene. Students then independently read the novel and completed the reading log as they finished each section. We stopped a few times during the reading to act out selected scenes. This process helped students to clarify any misunderstandings or confusing concepts in the text.

Writing

When most of the students had finished the novel, we began to write modified "I am" poems for Jesse Smoke, the main character and fictional author of the diary. I gave students the first words of eleven lines for the poem, and they used what they had learned about Jesse to complete the poem. Students had little trouble working independently to complete the poetry.

After we shared results, we revisited our prereading discussion about historical fiction and listed the names of the characters from the novel that were actual figures in the recorded story of the Trail of Tears. Students then worked with partners to write additional "I am" poems for those characters. This step was more challenging, so we turned to the historical notes at the end of the novel to clarify information.

Discussion

On an anticipation guide, I listed ten facts from the author's historical notes. Students checked whether they agreed or disagreed with the information based on what they remembered from the novel. They then independently read the notes, and we discussed the historical context of the novel. Students were then able to write in the voice of the historical figures.

Script Writing and Performance

As a class, we brainstormed key events from the novel and the historical notes that we would want included in a readers' theater script about the Trail of Tears. First I shared examples of historical readers' theater scripts with the students. Following the same format, students worked in small groups to write various scenes. They used the novel, the visitors' guide from the Cherokee reservation, and a few other print resources in order to write with greater accuracy. We shared the scenes in order of their occurrence. Six students volunteered to work with me outside of class to compile the "I am" poems and the short scripts into a cohesive readers' theater script, which we then shared with the social studies teacher.

Metacognition

I asked students to select from the following two prompts and write a short reflective essay on the novel study.

1. What do you now know about the Trail of Tears that you did not know before you read *The Journal of Jesse Smoke*? Write a short summary of that historical event as you explain your answer. How did reading the book help you? What other questions do you still have?

2. Consider each of the following activities we did during the novel study. Which was the easiest? Which was the most challenging? Which was the most engaging? Which ones would you recommend to the next group of students to study this book? Explain all of your answers.

   - Writing out scenes from the book
   - Writing "I am" poems for Jesse Smoke and historical figures
   - Writing a readers' theater script about the Trail of Tears.

Student Artifacts

I am Jesse Smoke, full-blooded Cherokee.
I saw our strong nation herded out of our land like sheep.
I heard sounds of pain and suffering along the weary trail.
I knew we would lose.
I didn't know like this.
I wonder what is in the future for our nation.
I believe the Cherokee nation will rise again like the phoenix.
This is my lifelong journal.
It symbolizes the power of my spirit and strength.
I wish our nation's willpower were stronger.
I am the full-blooded Cherokee, Jesse Smoke.

—Tobias

I am Andrew Jackson, the President of the United States.
I saw the Cherokee people fight along my side during the War of 1812.
I heard the Cherokee people cry.
I knew all about the Cherokee removal.
I did not know how much pain the Cherokee would be in.
I wonder why I turned on my fellow Cherokee friends John Ross and Sequoyah.
I believe I was wrong to do what I did in sponsoring the Removal Bill.
This is my pen.
It symbolizes all the pain I caused the Cherokee by signing the Removal Bill.
I wish I could turn back time and think with my heart.
I am Andrew Jackson, ex-president of the United States.

—Blanca

Teacher Reflection

Historical fiction can be challenging for students, especially if they have limited background knowledge or interest in the historical moment featured. Discussing the general history of the Trail of Tears before we read and the historical notes after most students had finished reading gave the students a better picture of the events we were studying.

Students were unable to complete the "I am" writing without first learning some basic information about the featured historical character. This need gave students a purpose for reading and researching, even texts that some found challenging. Many students reflected after the unit that the book became boring midway through. I don't believe this is true of all historical fiction, yet I do realize that many middle school students are accustomed to reading a story and getting a surprise ending. As we try to wean them away from short stories and into longer writing, we must expect them to experience moments of boredom and frustration due to their lack of background knowledge. This is the point where theater-related activities assist in "pushing" students through a novel.

All learning should involve an interactive activity, and theater is an easy way to implement that interaction. Visual, auditory, and kinesthetic learners benefit from activities that allow them to see, hear, and experience a subject. Drama is often the closest medium we have to "being there" through a historical moment, a scientific experiment, or a thought-provoking piece of literature.

In addition, art-based learning enhances the visualization process, which in turn supports strategic reading. The "I am" poems required students to "see" the character. The students then had to paint a picture of the character with words. As these poems were read aloud, listeners were able to visualize the characters as well.

Visualization is a necessary strategy for reading expository text. To help my students practice the strategy, I often read an illustrated book aloud to them, but I do not allow them to see the pictures. I stop after each page or so and ask students to create a brief sketch of what the author has painted with words. We then look at the illustrations and compare notes. What did we see or hear? Of course, this method works in reverse. Students can visualize their thoughts first and then use their sketches to write detailed exposition of what they want the reader to see through their writing.

With theater and illustrative arts, the possibilities are endless. What's most important is to make writing come alive for the reader and the writer.

Community ✦ Crossings

Suggestions on how you might adapt this lesson for a different classroom setting

- Literature teachers might use Lambert's strategies to encourage a close analysis of literary characters. Have students examine the actions of characters such as Macbeth or Julius Caesar and present their analyses using the "I am" framework. Or encourage students in social studies classes to cross time periods and similarly analyze the actions of historical figures.

- David Fitzgerald and Robert Conley's photo-essay book, *Cherokee*, could provide a prompt for recasting traditional text into performance text. Teachers of younger students would especially benefit from the vivid, detailed images of Cherokee life this book provides. In addition to an account of the Trail of Tears, Fitzgerald and Conley offer a view of contemporary Cherokee culture.

- Refer to Mimi Dyer's "Community Projects: Voices of the Trail" in the Community Projects section of the KCAC Web site (http://kcac.kennesaw.edu). Dyer's students drew on Diane Glancy's *Pushing the Bear* to create a dramatic text, effectively using their new knowledge of the Removal in a productive way.

8 Preserving the City

Bonnie G. Webb
Garrett Middle School, Austell, Georgia

Overview

This activity is based on the premise that students must "connect" to the city or community in which they live. What defines their area? What are the common bonds shared by all cities? What makes their city unique? What are the building blocks of their city? What does their city elect to preserve?

Philadelphia and Boston preserve artifacts honoring the Revolutionary War; Atlanta houses artifacts from the Civil War and the civil rights movement; Barrow, Alaska, hosts a museum to honor the art of whaling and the Inupiat culture. What a city, community, or family elects to preserve helps to define its culture.

School: Garrett Middle School
City: Austell, Georgia
Grade level: 8
Discipline: gifted social science
School setting: suburban
Number of students: 28
Students in school: 1,200

Time frame: This lesson can be expanded or shortened. As outlined below, the unit totaled fourteen in-school days, with a two-week window for students to complete their papers at home.

Objectives

Master objective: Students will produce a research paper that examines the culture of their city or community.

General objectives: Students are provided the opportunity to explore, research, and connect to a topic or issue that is close to home.

Research skill review: Students will revisit formal writing skills and enhance their general knowledge of their city.

Building Cities

Instructional Sequence

Students view a video that provides an overview of their city or general area. In whole-group discussion, the class lists what the film suggests are important aspects of the city. The class then defines the term *culture*. Basics include architecture, history, government, and transportation.

1. The teacher encourages students to look for the underlying, hidden, or ignored components of the city. Examples might include local family-run businesses, early professional sports teams, local heroes or events, authors, churches, civic organizations, town eccentrics, and the like.

2. The teacher prepares the bulletin board with the question "What defines the culture of a city?" and provides a variety of artifacts to get the students thinking and to demonstrate a balanced and varied selection.

3. Students bring in artifacts (picture, document, item). They should be encouraged to bring in something they connect with on a personal level. Students attach a caption describing their reason for the selection. The artifacts are shared and then displayed.

4. Students select artifacts to be researched. The student who contributed the artifact gets first choice of that artifact; students can also select one of the teacher-donated items.

5. Students then narrow (or focus) their topic or accept teacher-generated challenges for their selection.

   Examples:

   Photograph of Marietta, Georgia—The student focused on the history of Marietta Square.

   Atlanta Braves poster—The student accepted the teacher-provided challenge of researching Atlanta baseball before the Braves (Atlanta Black Crackers).

   Photo of the Winecoff Hotel fire—The student researched the worst hotel fire in the history of the United States.

   Street map of Savannah—The student narrowed the topic to the ghosts of Savannah.

   Photo of a barbershop opening (owned by the student's grandfather)—The student focused on the importance of community gathering places.

6. Review basic research paper instructions appropriate to the grade and ability level of the students.

7. Remind them to focus on the questions:

- How does your artifact define your city?
- Why is your topic important to the community?
- Why did your city elect to preserve your artifact?

8. Set timetable for research checkpoints, drafts, and final copy.

9. Present rubric (created by teacher, student, or both).

10. Students should have an abstract to share with the class the day the final draft is due.

11. Arrange time for student research.

Student Artifact

Excerpts from "Downtown Marietta, Georgia: Home of Southern Hospitality":

> In the heart of Marietta are the small shops and restaurants of the Marietta Square. There are the antique and specialty shops, the delis and other unique stores. What is now Dupree's Antique Shop, once was the local hardware and feed and seed store. These stores line the four streets surrounding Glover Park. The 1898 railroad station is now the Marietta Welcome Center. The rail lines are still in the same location as originally built in the 1840s. They are now the busiest rail lines in the country. The reason I chose this topic is that my family is often visiting the Square and other places in Marietta. I wanted to know about its founding and the effect it had on Georgia.

On December 19, 1834, Marietta was created by the Georgia legislature. The city is located in the Piedmont Plateau of North Central Georgia and northwest of the city of Atlanta. The town fathers honored Mary Cobb, wife of Senator Thomas W. Cobb, for whom the county was named. One of the earliest residents was James Anderson, the first postmaster of the town. He used the idea of a central square in the designing of Marietta, as he had in his hometown of Savannah, Georgia. . . .

One of the earliest houses built in Marietta was the Root House in 1845. It was built by William Root, who was a pharmacist originally from Philadelphia. The house was located on Church Street. Root was also one of the founders of the St. James Episcopal Church and served as county coroner. He was described as "very religious" and taught Sunday school. After Root's death in 1891, the house was moved back from Church Street and turned to face Lemon Street.

During the Civil War, the factories in Georgia supplied clothes and food for the Confederate Army. It stayed quiet until the spring of 1862, when twenty-two Union spies came to Marietta with the plan of stealing a locomotive and moving North, demolishing tracks, bridges, and tunnels on the way. . . .

During the chase, the General gave out and the northern raiders failed to destroy their main targets, the bridges over Chickamauga Creek, the Etowah River, and the tunnel at Tunnel Hill. This event in history has been dramatically reproduced in movies and is now known as "The Great Locomotive Chase.". . .

Another incident in Marietta's history has been made into a movie and the subject of many historical documentaries. Mary Phagan, a native of Marietta, moved to East Point and was working at the National Pencil Factory in Atlanta. Her murder in April of 1913 became known across the United States. Leo Frank, her Jewish manager, was convicted on eyewitness evidence provided by Jim Conley, once a suspect himself. Conley claimed that Frank made him help move the body of Mary Phagan to the basement and write the murder notes that were found at the scene of the crime. Frank was taken from the Georgia State Penitentiary in Milledgeville and lynched at the present-day corner of Frey's Gin and Roswell Road. In 1982, Alonzo Mann, an office boy at the factory admitted seeing Conley move the body by himself. This information led to [the] pardon of Frank in 1986. This incident was one of many that led to the rebirth of the Ku Klux Klan.

During World War II, Marietta's Rickenbacher Field served as home base for the Bell Bomber Factory. For four years the state-of-the-art field was used to test the bombers prior to flying them to the Western Front. State Representative James V. Carmichael and Marietta Mayor Rip Blair were the key people that persuaded Larry Bell to choose Marietta as the home for his factory. The plant employed 29,000 area men and women. The plant was rescued by Carmichael and the Lockheed Corporation in 1951, after being deserted by Bell. Through a number of name changes and consolidation, the facility is now known as Lockheed-Martin and is one of the top employers in the county and state.

New exclusive shopping areas such as the Cumberland Mall were built to accommodate the needs of the growing population. Gradually, the old shops around the Marietta Square became desolate. In the 1970s, a renewal effort began, inspired by Representative Howard Atherton and several others. A Downtown Marietta Authority was created to urge merchants and landlords to renovate their buildings, returning them to the way they had looked in the late 19th and early 20th centuries.

Throughout its time of existence, Marietta has felt the extremes of urban life: the degrading state of military occupation, brutal crimes, new developments, economic growth and decline. Although Marietta has had significant changes since 1834, it still manages to continue its tradition of extending warm Southern charm.

Bibliography
Cobb County. Spring 2001 <http://cobbcvb.com/>
Cobb OnLine. Spring 2001 <http://cobbonline.com/>
"A Journey Through Marietta Time." *Marietta Square.* Spring
    2001 <http://mariettasquare.com>
"Marietta 1833-2000." *Images of America.*
Marietta Square. Spring 2001 <http://mariettasquare.com>
North Georgia. Spring 2001 <http://ngeorgia.com/>
"Why was Marietta a Resort Center?" *Historical Highlights in
    Cobb County.*

—Ashley

Teacher Reflection

This activity provided an excellent opportunity for the students to relate better to the study of history and to be directly included in the planning of their work. Family and community involvement in the project evolved naturally into the activity and greatly enhanced both learning and classroom environments.

I introduced the activity with an artifact of my own. A Bible that belonged to my late mother has a special place in our family. My great-grandfather was a Bible guilder. His job was to apply gold to the edges of the pages. Bible guilding, now a lost art, was a high-level job at the A. J. Holman Bible Company in the 1930s. PopPop walked this particular Bible through all the stages of production, making the entire Bible on his own. The students were interested in both the Bible and the story of its importance. After hearing the story, they realized this was not a typical Bible. I encouraged them to bring in an artifact that had special meaning for either them or their family. I stressed family more than self to keep the number of teddy bears and baby blankets to a minimum.

Some of the artifacts were valuable, so we photographed those items and returned them home immediately. One artifact was so special that the parent brought it to school to be photographed. He didn't want to risk it being damaged on the bus or in the book bag.

The students then created a bulletin board display of the class work. They also included staged photographs of the process and the presentations. This bulletin board was a student idea, and several students brought in photographs of local landmarks to display. Some of the images they provided were more than fifty years old. These were scanned and the originals returned to their owners.

The time allotted for this project was originally one month, with other curriculum-related activities included. I wanted to give the students adequate time to find a suitable artifact and to research primary and secondary sources. This time frame proved to be too long and was shortened. The shorter period allowed us to sustain our enthusiasm. It also kept the project more compact and easier for me to direct.

I underestimated class enthusiasm for the project. I think that the students' great attitude developed because they could incorporate their own lives into the project. Since we were "writing the book," they also were allowed to suggest, comment on, and sometimes change assignments. I learned that class ownership of the project is essential for student involvement.

Surprisingly, the proofreading phase of the activity brought most of the parents into it. Some parents helped their children select their artifacts, but more became involved after reading the first draft of their child's report. The proof sheet required an adult's signature on the first draft. Many parents added comments for their children to include on the revision.

I found the students' reaction to their peers' projects a little disappointing. Most seemed interested only in their own projects. In future endeavors, I will include writing partnerships or peer-group readings from the start to encourage interest in the writing of others.

Community ✤ Crossings

Suggestions on how you might adapt this lesson for a different classroom setting

- Have students use a variety of texts to examine what their city or town has chosen to highlight or preserve about its history: historical markers, tourism pamphlets, the local history museum, or historic structures that have been preserved. Students could then analyze why those particular topics (e.g., Civil War, Trail of Tears) have been highlighted. As an extension, students could analyze which parts of history have been overlooked and why.

- Encourage students to explore the ways in which a city aims to build a new identity through establishing new institutions. The high school students in Dave Winter's American literature class (see Chapter 11, "My Classroom Really Is a Zoo"), for example, examined how Atlanta civic leaders sought to build a reputation for Atlanta as an international metropolitan center by creating a world-class zoo.

- Students could also document their town or city as they experience it on a day-to-day basis (consider modifying the photography project outlined in Chapter 4, "Viewfinders: Students Picturing Their Communities") and then compare different perspectives. Students could then analyze what should be preserved, protected, or created based on *their* experiences. As an extension of this project, students could compare their conclusions to what other historical agents or agencies have chosen to preserve about the city. Are the perspectives simply generational?

- Have students analyze which historical periods are most represented in local history museums, brochures, and the like. Then have them formulate how to fill in gaps, investigating larger historical trends and more local historical topics. Ultimately, students could produce a historical exhibit—or historical marker projects—that help highlight untold stories.

- Allow students to explore the importance of material culture and how these artifacts *collectively* tell a story. Students could collect artifacts around one central topic (e.g., their town, baseball, after-school activities) and then examine as a group what these artifacts say about the topic and/or about why civic leaders or citizens keep them.

- Incorporate a geographic element by having the students and/or people they interview draw maps of their city, town, or neighborhood (whatever the chosen subject is). The cartographers should be asked to include and label buildings, streets, or areas (school, ball fields, places they played) they remember from a particular time period. Students could then analyze the maps.

9 Recovering Displaced Heritages in Multiple Contexts

Linda Templeton
East Paulding High School, Dallas, Georgia

Overview

As an English educator, I want my students to write literature-based essays and to take ownership of their writing. No matter what subjects we teach, most of us want our students to write well about the subject matter we teach. But does this happen 100 percent of the time? 75 percent? 50 percent? 10 percent? Through this project, I discovered a way to hook my first-year students as readers and writers, encouraging interesting essays by combining creativity and analytical writing. After reading Elie Wiesel's *Night,* Robert Conley's *Mountain Windsong,* and Diane Glancy's *Pushing the Bear,* completing several activities, and having many discussions, students wrote an essay for the final evaluation of the unit. My objective was to have them read the selections, write an essay centered on their close examination of displaced heritages within different historical periods, and draw conclusions as to the similarities between these seemingly unrelated events in history.

> **School:** East Paulding High School
> **City:** Dallas, Georgia
> **Grade level:** 9
> **Discipline:** honors literature/composition
> **School setting:** rural
> **Number of students:** 40
> **Students in school:** 1,200

Instructional Sequence

All of my students read Elie Wiesel's *Night* because his text provided the foundation for our unit theme of displaced heritages. Students dealt with thought-provoking questions, delving into the heart of the text. Because I wanted them to move into the other two books, *Mountain Windsong* and *Pushing the Bear,* I did not want our theme to focus exclusively on the Holocaust. I wanted my students to be able to see and understand the idea of displaced heritages as a thread connecting the three selections.

Reclaiming Displaced Heritages

Because I didn't have enough copies of *Mountain Windsong* and *Pushing the Bear*, I divided students into two groups: one group read *Mountain Windsong* and the other group read *Pushing the Bear.* We held whole-group discussions with students listening and learning about the book they were not reading. Also, small-group discussions allowed students to discuss events from the texts that they felt were interesting or confusing or that they just needed to discuss. As a teacher, I became the facilitator, rotating among the groups, listening to their discussions, and answering questions.

As a class, we examined the then-unfinished play *Where the Deer Ran: Events Leading to the Cherokee Removal* by Kennesaw State University graduate student Adam Russell. Students participated in performing the play and then offered suggestions to the playwright. After critiquing the play, students wrote their own miniplays, basing them on a scene or event from *Mountain Windsong* or *Pushing the Bear,* and then performed the plays for their classmates. I encouraged them to keep in mind their suggestions for *Where the Deer Ran,* hoping they would incorporate these suggestions into their own creative plays. To aid in their playwriting adventure, students researched the Trail of Tears to add missing information or answer questions that had arisen during this activity. I required a short written piece about the subject of their research, complete with bibliography, and students had to present their findings to the class.

After the reading, discussing, researching, playwriting, and performing, students wrote a reflective essay as the final evaluation piece for this unit. During a whole-class brainstorming session, we created the following topics for their essays:

1. Changing lives
2. Symbolism of the bear
3. Relationships
4. Choices people make
5. Love's enduring power
6. Compare/contrast *Night* with *Pushing the Bear*
7. Using one of the quotes from the Holocaust unit, correlate the quote with the novel read (see the following quotations):

Those who cannot remember the past are doomed to repeat it.

—Santayana

I felt and feel it was not German [substitute White] man I had met, but man. He, under certain conditions, be I.

—Anonymous

The only thing necessary for the triumph of evil is for good men to do nothing.

—Edmund Burke (1774)

Somebody should do something. Then I realized I am somebody.

—Anonymous

To sin by silence when they should protest, makes cowards of men.

—Abraham Lincoln

We were not six million [substitute 14,000], we were Yitzaks and Sarahs [substitute Maritoles and Knobowtees], and we were like trees whose limbs were cut off one at a time.

—Otto Kraus

Silence may be golden, but may also be yellow.

—Anonymous

An eye for an eye and a tooth for a tooth leaves the world toothless and blind.

—Anonymous

The killing of one is murder; after that it's just statistics.

—Stalin

Hear the voices, see the signs, for you are the promise of a new spring in the forest of the world.

—Anonymous

The hottest places in hell are reserved for those who, in times of moral crisis, maintain their neutrality.

—Dante

If I am for myself, who will be for me? And if I am for myself alone, who am I? If not now, when?

—Rabbi Hillel

Most of all, I wanted my students to undertake a close examination of displaced heritages within different historical periods and to identify the similarities between these seemingly unrelated events in history.

Student Artifact

The book *Mountain Windsong* tells the tale where the quote "Hear the voices, see the signs, for you are the promise of a new spring in the forest of the world" leaves off. The voices, signs, and sagas lead Chooj to believe that he is the new spring in the forest of the Cherokee world, meaning he will live life the modern way, but respect life through Cherokee lives and stories. Chooj's grandfather could have told him this quote because he is really trying to relay information and the heritage of his ancestors to him.

The "voices" form a love song that Oconeechee and Whipoorwill sing to each other. The "signs" refer to the trails, culture, and heritage left behind by the Cherokee. Chooj learns that his life is not only his, but the future of the forest, the Cherokee people. The grandfather is almost in the winter of life, so he sheds his seeds of knowledge on fertile soil (Chooj), who will bloom into new life for the Cherokee.

Chooj's life now will noticeably undergo a change, almost like a metamorphosis. He will become a person that will not make the same mistakes of his ancestors because he is learning from them. Chooj will now be used as a showcase for the Cherokee nation to the world of other nations. Chooj will intertwine the lessons from the old and new to help him develop into a man, learning from his past and knowing his future. At the same time the other boys and girls in his day will bloom also, proving to themselves that as long as they preserve the past, their culture will remain as beautiful and united as the wildflowers on the prairies.

—Leon

Teacher Reflection

Leon's completed essay was one of his best writings of the entire school year. He chose to apply one of the quotes from the Holocaust unit to Robert Conley's *Mountain Windsong*. When I noticed his perusal of the Holocaust unit quotes, my heart skipped a beat because I too would have chosen that particular activity for my essay. Secretly I was hoping that if other students noticed Leon examining the quotes, they would go that route too; out of forty students, however, Leon was the only one to choose this essay topic. Also, Leon's strengths as a creative writer surpassed his abilities as an analytical writer, so by choosing this particular essay topic he was able to incorporate his creative writing skills into an analytical essay. As he progressed with writing the essay, he asked me to read it over; we had worked collaboratively during the year, trying to improve his writing as a whole, so he had come full circle, recognizing the value of feedback. When I read the first few sentences, tears rushed to my eyes. In his own way, Leon had found the quote that bridged the two historical incidences—Holocaust and Cherokee Removal—intertwining the two beautifully. He had captured the essence of this assignment. When I gained control of my emotions, I let him know that he was on target with his writing and told him to finish it, making few changes. I'll never forget how Leon beamed with pride when he received his A for the essay, but more than anything, he loved having me read his essay to the entire class. In fact, he asked me to read his paper to the class; I didn't have to ask him.

After hearing Leon's essay, the students congratulated him on a job well done, but more important, they let him know they were amazed by the way he had aligned the quote with the text. I think it also made them sorry they hadn't chosen that topic. Sharing Leon's paper with the class led the other students to investigate how many of the other quotes also related to *Mountain Windsong* and *Pushing the Bear*. Leon's moment in the spotlight had lasting effects because he gained confidence in himself as a writer and stopped moaning and groaning when given an essay assignment.

For me, this activity proved the value of giving students essay topic choices. I realize that creative writing cannot always be incorporated with analytical writing, but I do feel that if teachers stepped outside the box more often, they could find essay topics that appeal to more than one of the strengths of student writers. First-year high school writers often are not equipped with that critical eye for analyzing a piece of literature. Through creative writing assignments, teachers enable young writers to develop their critical-thinking abilities. This particular writing activity evolved over a period of time while we were reading and exploring the selections. I gave my students choices, something all teachers should allow when possible. If I had given the usual ho-hum essay writing choices, Leon probably could not have produced such high-quality writing. His creative eye enabled him to analyze the reading assignment and then correlate the poetic quote, bridging the two genres. I will always remember Leon's paper and will probably use it as an example when teaching this unit again.

Community ✣ Crossings

Suggestions on how you might adapt this lesson for a different classroom setting

- This activity would work well as a partnership with world history and American history classrooms. Two teachers could work collaboratively on a unit in which students are divided into reading groups to read the different selections. After completing the readings, students would then work collaboratively to examine both historical events, looking for examples of displaced heritages. Also, an English teacher could team-teach this unit with a history teacher and have the students write the essays after their collaborations.

- The causes of historical events that create displaced peoples could be examined in classrooms ranging from a university environmental science course to a high school government classroom. Science students might examine how shifts in environmental conditions have forced groups of peoples to relocate. Government classes could focus on the politics that commonly create forced exiles like the Japanese internment in the United States or the African diaspora.

- In disciplines other than English, culminating products for this unit could take different forms: a collection of maps indicating movement patterns and destinations, a dramatic performance drawing on oral histories, charts and graphs indicating and comparing qualitative information about each historical event.

- Rather than reading novels for source material, students might locate and read current or historic records of displacement within the United States and internationally. Accessing international newspapers online <www.world-newspapers.com> to research displaced heritages within other countries would provide students with a global perspective on the scope and repercussions of displacement.

- This unit provides a framework that uniquely suits the exploration of ethics and values within any discipline, from character education in an elementary school to an advanced medical program. An examination of displacement reveals the personal and public conflicts within these movements. A unit could be structured conceptually (gentrification) or around communities (migrant farmworkers, "Doctors without Borders"). Most teachers will find this unit an ideal framework for providing opportunities for research into real-life questions and situations about exiled or displaced persons.

IV Extended Research Projects

10 Hometown History: The Hickory Flat Oral History Project

Peggy Maynard Corbett
Sequoyah High School, Canton, Georgia

Overview

The Hickory Flat Oral History Project began as a simple plan to interview older members of our community in an effort to preserve the stories of those who had witnessed life in an agricultural area during the early years of the twentieth century. Discussions about our community and its changing face illustrated that there was much to value in a past that we now only faintly remember. Students began to realize that it was impossible to value what we did not know or understand and that their lives and their roles in their community might be enriched if they had a clearer picture of what had come before them. They were also able to acknowledge that communities continually redefine themselves in relation to other cultural phenomena.

> The class members who participated in this inquiry were senior English students at Sequoyah High School in Canton, Georgia. Sequoyah is in the rural community of Hickory Flat, although its student body is evenly distributed between local rural students and suburban transplants to the area. The school consists of about 1,450 students, with a very low percentage of minority students.

Cultivating Homelands

The students discovered that authentic research is an inquiry process rather than merely a paper product. With the guidance of the local Historical Society, the students decided that a documentary could be produced from Hickory Flat's stories. They believed that an audience larger than themselves would value the stories and that video might provide an accessible venue for that purpose.

The project was ongoing and multifaceted. Individual students performed many tasks over the course of the assignment. They generated inquiry questions; read texts that illustrated their concepts; set and adjusted deadlines; evaluated documentaries; practiced time management; used a variety of writing modes to adjust style, voice, and purpose; and practiced editing skills in practically every phase of the project.

The assignment included the following components:

- Interview a resident of Hickory Flat who has lived here his or her entire life and who was born prior to 1940.
- Transcribe the taped interview.
- Using the transcription, write a first-person narrative from the interview subject's point of view.

A group of student volunteers also used the narratives to create a script for the video.

Instructional Sequence

The project grew out of a class discussion of nonfiction reading assignments from "Coming to Terms with Place" (McQuade and McQuade) and *Crabgrass Frontier: The Suburbanization of the United States* (Jackson). Our study of community and place in general, and our own community and place specifically, led to a discussion of the architectural structures familiar to all farm communities, and students expressed disappointment that many of Hickory Flat's structures, vestiges of the area's rich agricultural past, were disappearing. I reminded them that the disappearance of a structure was no reason to forget that it had ever been there or that it had played a role in a great story. Seizing the moment, I had students read an excerpt from Raymond Andrews's *The Last Radio Baby* titled "The Farm." We discussed its relevance to our own community, and several students mentioned that their grandparents, who had grown up in Hickory Flat, had related similar stories to them. I read to the class a corresponding chapter from Jimmy Carter's *An Hour before Daylight*, and we discussed the fact that race, geography, age, and economics fundamentally altered the experiences shared by farm families during the early and mid-twentieth century. From there the students concluded that, like area structures, many of the local residents were disappearing, along with their stories, and the students decided to make collecting and documenting these stories their research project.

The first assignment was to prepare for an interview. After we read the Andrews and Carter excerpts, I assigned students the task of creating a list of possible inquiry questions. We used the text from the two memoirists to determine the types of information we would need in order to illustrate what life on a farm in our area was like. After a discussion of their questions and the problems students might encounter, we planned for a trial run. I invited Mr. Wilson, a former teacher and lifelong Hickory Flat resident, to visit the class for a group interview. Students taped the interview, and the next day we listened to it and discussed problems that arose and how they had dealt with them, addressing ways to avoid some of those pitfalls. With Mr. Wilson's and my help, the students were paired with Hickory Flat interview subjects. They were given a month to arrange the interview, transcribe the tape, and type up the transcription.

The next step involved turning the transcripts into narratives. I again used the Andrews and Carter texts, this time to illustrate what a narrative was and the components and tools of narrative writing. I also transcribed an interview tape and provided sections of the transcripts to student groups for them to write up as a narrative. The next day we listened to their narratives, peer edited, and discussed what worked and what did not. Additional practice in composing inquiry questions and writing the results in narrative form were provided through an excerpt from *The Last Radio Baby* and through interviewing their classmates. Each interview required students to focus on a single topic and to shape the narrative to tell of a specific event, custom, or experience. The class decided to write all of the narratives in first person in order to preserve the voices of the interview subjects.

Finally students were ready to turn their interview transcripts into narratives. They were relieved to know they would not have to use every word of the transcripts in the narratives. I allowed one week for rough drafts. At that time, we peer edited, read drafts aloud, and sent them back for revisions. Our plan was to collect the narratives into a book, but the president of the Historical Society visited in the meantime and gave us the idea of creating a documentary film. This suggestion energized my students. After investigating funding sources and receiving support from the state humanities council, the students forged ahead with the plan. Rather than involve the entire class in this part of the project, I first asked if any students were interested in volunteering to work on the script. Three students immediately volunteered based on their interest in film. Involving small groups of volunteers in various tasks seemed preferable to trying to coordinate an entire class on one task. The other students helped by making phone calls and writing press announcements aimed at collecting artifacts for the digital background.

As a starting point, the script committee pored over pages of transcriptions and read the narratives. From there they literally cut and pasted, organizing the material into categories that included farm, school, church, and community life and ending with a piece on the 1830 Worley–Quarles farmhouse. Using pictures and other artifacts collected during the interview process and through later small-group efforts, the script committee organized the information around those artifacts and prepared the script for the video production company.

Following is the written list of requirements I gave the students early in the project:

- Copies of all writing you have generated in planning and executing the project, to include project descriptions, journals, letters, meeting notes, reflections, online bulletin board postings, practice interviews and narratives, etc.
- Your mid-project reflection piece that explains your initial perceptions and how they have evolved throughout the process
- One journal entry per week posted online and a copy for your portfolio, in which you discuss progress, frustrations, incidences, experiences, etc.
- A copy of your interview transcripts
- A copy of your final narrative
- A final reflection piece
- Your self-evaluation rubric
- A disk with your interview transcripts and narratives

Although the project began spontaneously and therefore without any focus on the grading process, I realized that eventually I would have to assess students' work. These materials served as assessment guidelines.

Student Artifact

Below is an excerpt from the script, "Life in Twentieth-Century Hickory Flat," created from the class narratives. The script committee read narratives, cut and pasted by category, selected photographs, and prepared a storyboard for the videographer.

Narrator: Six miles southwest of Canton, Georgia, in Cherokee County, lies Hickory Flat, which was founded around 1820. After the evacuation of the Cherokee Indians, the land was sold through a government land lottery. In the early days, it was mentioned as a possible county seat, but that position passed over Hickory Flat and that honor was given to the city of Canton. The settlers who purchased the land named it Hickory Flat for the numerous hickory trees growing on the vast flat spaces. Since its founding, Hickory Flat has been a thriving, prosperous, and developing area. A close-knit and friendly community, it has focused on agriculture, education, and religion to build up to what it has become.

First Character: Swine and cattle were the primary livestock raised here. Almost every family in Hickory Flat owned a cow up until the '50s. We depended on them for milk and butter for bartering, especially when the Depression came, when it was hard for everyone to make a living on the farm. I remember going to the general store at the corner with my mother when I was young. Since we had little money, my mother and I bartered eggs and a few chickens for items we could not raise ourselves, such as flour, meal, sugar, and coffee. The only cash crops in Hickory Flat were corn and cotton. When I was old enough, I would wake up before dawn to work the fields of cotton, which was the single most important cash crop in the county at the time. In autumn, my family and I would gather the large amounts of cotton to take to the cotton gin for processing. There was only one cotton gin in Hickory Flat, and it unfortunately burned down in the 1940s, bringing the cotton industry down with it. My father took what money we had left from our cotton farming and built a chicken house and bought a few dozen chickens, which we used for eggs and meat. We gradually joined the booming poultry industry in the South along with many of our neighbors, and Georgia eventually became the biggest and most important poultry raising state in the nation. After a few years, many more farmers continued to join the poultry industry, and eventually the surplus of chickens became too great for the small Hickory Flat economy to handle. As prices plummeted, most chicken farmers sold their chickens to larger corporations such as Seaboard Farms in Canton, and the independent farmers began to disappear from the county.

Second Character: The Hickory Flat School started out as a one-room building in 1838. There was a large fireplace in one corner of the room that was used to heat the school. The boys would usually help chop wood to feed the stove. There was no indoor plumbing so that meant no bathrooms. Girls used one side of the woods and the boys would use the other. We sat on long benches with no tops and wrote on slates with chalk because there was no paper. School was held for five months in the winter and two in the summer, so the kids would be free to help their families for spring planting and fall harvesting. Eventually the school built on additional rooms and we got desks, which were much more comfortable, and they made it easier to write. When other schools started to be built in the 1950s, the Hickory Flat community raised money and built a gymnasium in an effort to keep their little school open. Fifty years later children are still playing ball in that same gym. A cafeteria was also built from an old army barrack in the late '40s. It had no formal equipment, just old wooden tables. All the dishes were washed by hand. Before the cafeteria, students would go home around noon to eat lunch. One time, the community canned food during the harvesting so that the school cafeteria had food for the students. The people of Hickory Flat always worked together for the good of the community. . . .

Fourth Character: The Worley–Quarles house has stood watch over the Hickory Flat community for around 170 years. We can only imagine what the crossroads looked like in the 1830s when she was in her infancy. We do know that one couldn't walk without hearing the constant crunch of the plentiful hickory nuts that gave the area its name. . . . Over a period of many years, the house has witnessed incredible changes. Mules and wagons gave way to automobiles, dirt roads to paved ones, cotton fields to chicken houses, and general stores succumbed to supermarkets. During all of these shifts, however, the Worley–Quarles house has stood vigil. . . . Our children today know it only in its faded form, as a place that has always been there marking the spot at the crossroads. It reassures them with its quiet dignity and its constancy in their ever-changing lives and landscapes.

Narrator: Hickory Flat has obviously changed greatly over the years, as is expected by any growing community. Despite the changes, however, it remains a tightly bonded community of good people who are determined to work together to better the place they call home.

—created by Rachael, Ashley, and Teresa

Student Reflection

This project has made me realize that knowing a little more about my community has given me more respect for it and makes me realize how unappreciative I have been of my surroundings and culture. I no longer take for granted the community that has seen me grow up and which I have seen grow bigger. I see now that there is a rich culture here and that it's not just a place where old crabby geezers just want to chew your ear off all day. I have begun to see these people as intelligent and experienced in ways that I'm not yet and to realize the value of knowing your neighbors and your community. In learning about Hickory Flat I know the land better and know that it breathes a thousand tales. I no longer look at my place as a mirror of every other town in America, but rather as a portrait of a personal and touchable group of souls that have sweated, worked, laughed, and cried together, and a place that is uniquely mine.

—Bill

Teacher Reflection

I would be less than honest if I didn't say that I worked harder in facilitating this project than I have ever worked in my life. But I can also say with complete honesty that this project and the work my students did have provided me with an enormous sense of accomplishment and pride and been worth every minute I spent. It is not easy to juggle a project of this magnitude with all the other details a teacher must attend to each day; it is much easier to stay inside the box and use the book and familiar manuals. But knowing that my students were engaged in learning that also provided opportunities for character development and that directly connected them to their community made it worthwhile. They received a great deal from the people they worked with and from being involved in meaningful research. In spite of the myriad difficult details we had to manage every day, the work students did will remain with them long after standard curriculum objectives have faded.

Several years after the students who undertook the Hickory Flat project graduated, I received the following unsolicited e-mail message from Allison, a member of that class:

> I feel I learned tons about literature and writing in your class, but I really got the most out of the Hickory Flat project. I had a cultural experience, really saw life (and Canton) from a different perspective, and really felt that something I had done in high school, for a class, really mattered. I not only learned "stuff," but I felt like I learned about people and life. The reflections you had us do, and the poems and other things you had us examine really brought me to an understanding of things besides literary elements, and that takes something special to be able to incorporate both knowledge and life (heart stuff) into the classroom.

Allison's reflection confirmed what I had suspected all along: my students' pride in their work provided a great motivation during the project and left a lasting impression after it. I set the deadlines and the objectives students were required to meet for their grade, but the momentum in their work was an element I don't usually see. They monitored their progress, never asked about grades, discussed their activities with one another and with me, discussed the project at home and in church, made suggestions, asked questions, and genuinely cared about the outcome. Such involvement is what we all dreamed about when we decided to become teachers. The key to the success of a project like this is ownership—student ownership of the project and the outcome. When I stopped owning their learning experiences, my students became true learners.

Community ✤ Crossings

Suggestions on how you might adapt this lesson for a different classroom setting (this unit has natural crossover value)

- A U.S. history teacher could use the principles and activities of this project in a number of twentieth-century units. A study of the Great Depression, World War II, or the Vietnam War would benefit from this type of personal inquiry.

- Art teachers or video technology teachers could create projects using the principles of research and reporting developed here. Murals and documentaries are natural media for documenting place and time. Sociology teachers could also create units about community and the individual's place in it.

- Younger students might begin to recover the history of their community by bringing in and analyzing old photographs of the community (see Chapter 4, "Viewfinders: Students Picturing Their Communities"). Alternatively, students could examine contemporary photographs of their community, identifying elements that would not have existed sixty years before and noting elements no longer present.

- This project could easily be adapted to recover histories other than those of rural and agricultural communities. Students in an urban environment, for example, might address the impact of gentrification; suburban students might investigate the growth of suburbia and focus their research on why and how their community has evolved.

- Students might also use such hands-on investigation of their community to become active citizens in it by focusing their research on current community issues or problems. Student groups could interview local citizens, policymakers, and experts, as well as participate in relevant events and activities, all in preparation for proposing a solution and a call to action. Final projects could be presented to classmates and/or community leaders. Projects could take various forms, such as PowerPoint presentations or Web sites.

11 My Classroom Really Is a Zoo (What We Did and What I Wish We Had Done)

Dave Winter
Wheeler High School, Marietta, Georgia

Overview

From the beginning, this project involved three communities: (1) the cultural community (real or imagined) of metropolitan Atlanta, (2) the scholarship community of the Keeping and Creating American Communities program, and (3) the classroom community I hoped to create. Throughout this project and through my efforts to sustain it in the years since, my students have consistently been funda-mental shapers of both the final product of our work and the pro-cess by which we arrived at it.

School: Wheeler High School
City: Marietta, Georgia
Grade level: 11
Discipline: honors American literature
School setting: suburban to urban
Number of students: 20
Students in school: 1,700

Their enthusiasm for engaging both the cultural community around them and the scholarship community of the KCAC program remains one of the greatest discoveries and greatest joys of my teaching career.

Building Cities

My original goal was to investigate the his-tory of a cultural space in metropolitan Atlanta. The broader goal: to determine the identity of Atlanta by studying what it elects to preserve. By preserv-ing this building, or that museum, or this stadium, or that park, the urban community (or any commu-nity, for that matter) must assert its central values, announcing to themselves and to those outside the community: "This is what we are all about. This is who we are as a com-munity." My colleagues, the original members of the Building Cities teacher inquiry team, identified this critical approach and some places in the city where we might apply it (the High Museum of Art, the King Center, the Carter Center's Presidential Library and Museum, and the World of Coca-Cola).

Armed with these choices and the broader theme of Building Cities, I approached my senior AP Language and Composition class with the proposal that we conduct the study as a class project. The theme piqued their interest. The proposed cultural spaces did not.

"Why don't we do the zoo?" proposed Meredith, with a mix of genuine enthusiasm and uncertainty about how I would react. I think she expected me to chastise her for being frivolous and juvenile. After pausing to consider the idea, I surprised her by announcing that it was a perfect choice. The zoo is one place where a city creates itself, and the history of Atlanta's zoo is in many ways the history of the city in microcosm. Equally important, the zoo is a fun subject to study. It was the perfect marriage: a serious process that investigated a fun subject.

Unfortunately for Meredith and her senior peers, we never got around to visiting and researching the zoo that fall. A time-consuming schoolwide senior project and preparation for the AP exam (all in a semester course) caused me to postpone the project until the spring semester, when a precocious class of honors eleventh graders entered my classroom to take American literature. Ultimately it was they who inherited and completed this Building Cities project, determining subtopics for research, conducting oral histories with key zoo employees, and writing I-Search papers about their discoveries.

Two principles underline the work I assigned these students. Although I wanted their work to be as rigorous as a traditional literary-based research paper, I also wanted them to understand that research is ultimately a collaborative process. A "real" researcher works in a community of scholarship, each scholar relying on and amplifying the research that existed before he or she entered the conversation. Too often, high school research paper assignments fail to distinguish between true collegiality in research and plagiarism. The effort (legitimate and illegitimate) spent cheating on research papers and preventing cheating on research papers is a depressing subject. Rather than being a patrolman in the plagiarism police force, I decided to create a research project for which the bulk of the research was primary (interviews, newspaper articles, photographs). To make the research process collegial, though, my students and I created a pool of resources that all students could access: one pool was a classroom archives; the other was an Internet archive that contained all of the photographs and interviews the class had taken or conducted. We invited four photographers from the school newspaper staff to accompany us on our site visit to the zoo. The photos they took for us became the photo archive the students used to illustrate the text of their I-Search papers. The students were encouraged to depend on their own research and the research of classmates to write their papers.

The second principle is that we would try to create something useful for the broader community we were researching. By pursuing this goal, I was trying to encourage my classroom community to join the larger metropolitan community, not only by considering that larger community's identity but also by helping to preserve it and expand it while creating new resources available to the zoo and to other teachers.

Instructional Sequence

Note: This sequence of activities can be adapted to the study of cultural landmarks in any city.

1. Discuss the theme of Building Cities with the class. Suggest the class do research papers on part of the city instead of traditional research papers involving fun-filled trips to the library to look through reference books for hours.

2. Brainstorm possible sites that have helped (or failed to help) forge an (inter)national identity for the city.

3. Brainstorm possible end products that might come out of such a collaborative research process.

4. Find a film or an article that presents the history of the place/site you intend to cover. The film or article serves as an introduction to the place and will be useful for coming up with subtopics for students to research individually or in teams.

5. During a whole-class discussion, brainstorm a list of subtopics the class will then research.

6. Have students embark on a quest for newspaper and magazine articles that touch on the subtopics the class brainstormed. I sought volunteers and bribed them with extra credit, but you could easily make it an assignment for each student in the class.

7. Using the same list of research topics, have students submit their top three research choices and then assign those topics so that all subtopics are covered.

8. Conduct a field trip to the study site. During this trip, students should take copious notes of their observations and plenty of photos of the site. The observations and the photos are valuable resources for the research papers at project's end. (I would be remiss if I didn't thank Zoo Atlanta's Education Department

for hosting a wonderful experience during our field trip. They allowed my students access to old, confining habitats that have since been converted to more humane uses. Seeing and comparing the old and new habitats was a powerful experience, and it contributed greatly to the success of our project.)

9. After you get the film developed or create files of digital images, have students volunteer to write captions for the photos. The photo forms we developed included space for a caption, a space to name the photographer for photo credit, and a place to rank the photo's overall usefulness and quality.

10. Have students brainstorm a list of potential interview subjects and then have students sign up in pairs to interview particular subjects. The pairing of students helped to limit both the number of subjects (thereby keeping them relevant) and the students' inhibitions.

11. Prepare students for their interview by teaching them different interview techniques. I wanted students to craft their interviews into a final piece, so I used models in Studs Terkel's book *Working* and Rick Ayers's companion text *Studs Terkel's Working: A Teaching Guide.* The idea was for students to have three options for presenting their interview: simple Q-and-A, the journalistic personality feature, and the Studs Terkel-esque oral history.

12. Compile an archive of photographs, articles, and interviews so that people can check them out. I again gave copious extra credit to a student who served as our class archivist. The student organized the documents and photos into folders so that students could check them out on a daily basis.

13. Post all resources to a classroom Web site as another way to make the research available. This provided a twenty-four-hour resource for all students with computers. The interviews were posted in both raw transcript form and final transcript form. I received final transcripts in all three interview formats, but most were in question-and-answer format.

14. Have each student compose a research paper on his or her subtopic using the I-Search format. First-person narration is okay, as is a narrative description. Trust me, these papers are much more enjoyable for the teacher to read and for the students to write.

    Sample I-Search Structure:

    a. What I Knew (and Didn't Know) about My Topic When I Began.

    b. Why I'm Writing This Paper. Here's where a real need should reveal itself; the writer demonstrates that the search may make a difference in his or her life.

    c. The Search—the narrative of the hunt.

    d. What I Learned (or Didn't Learn). A search that failed can be as exciting and valuable as one that succeeds.

15. Complete one or more whole-class projects. Some good ideas include a class anthology, a fictional book aimed at young readers, and a model of the site being studied that illustrates its change over time. We never did any of these ☹. We ran out of time.

Student Artifact

Excerpts from "The Pandas of Zoo Atlanta: An I-Search Paper"

I never really saw what the big deal was about the zoo. . . . Frankly, I couldn't see what everyone was getting so excited about. When I thought about zoos, all I pictured was a bunch of foul-smelling animals with millions of screaming kids running around. I remember my dad telling me how much I loved the zoo as a child and how he would take me every Sunday morning, but I had no recollection of such a thing. Sure, I was glad to be missing a day of school, but I didn't see it as anything more than that.

When I began thinking about topics to research, the pandas immediately came to mind. I remembered how the press had made a huge deal about their arrival, and although I had no idea why, I was mildly curious. I figured they would be an easy topic to write about. After all, the zoo had very recently acquired them, and they were pretty darn cute. My 8-year-old brother had come back from Zoo Atlanta raving about Lun-Lun and Yang-Yang, so I thought to myself, how hard could it be? . . .

It was [during our field trip to] Zoo Atlanta that my outlook completely changed. Our class was lucky enough to see many of the former animal habitats, and they really made an impression on everyone, including myself. In the primate house, the living areas were made entirely out of glass and concrete; there wasn't a plant in sight [Figure 11.1]. Most of the cages were smaller than my bathroom. It was truly heartbreaking, and it seemed unbelievable that living creatures were subjected to such horrifying treatment only 15 years ago. The contrast between their former and present living conditions was astonishing. It gave me a whole new level of appreciation and respect for the zoo. . . .

When we finally arrived at the highlight of the trip, the pandas, I instantly fell in love with them. How could you not? They were the cutest things I ever saw. One of them was sleeping, and the other was eating bamboo. They looked like overgrown stuffed animals. Everywhere people were captivated by the awesome mammals, and I could actually feel myself getting excited about

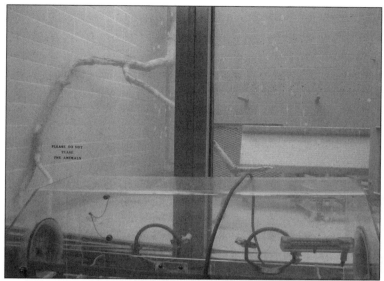

Figure 11.1: An empty cage in the old Primate Building is still used for storage or for temporary holding for new animals. In the foreground is an incubator. (Photo by Ashley Kruythoff, caption by Brett Younker.)

researching their journey to Zoo Atlanta. I even bought Terry Maple's book *Saving the Giant Panda* to help me with my paper. The book proved to be a worthy investment since it outlined the panda's expedition to Atlanta from the very beginning. It was at this point that I finally believed there was a greater purpose to this assignment.

After my "revelation," I was ready to put some effort into the paper. My interview partner, Bennett Golder, and I began to try and contact the director of Zoo Atlanta, the aforementioned Dr. Terry Maple. Maple had transformed Zoo Atlanta from one of the worst zoos in the nation to one of the best. He had also played a critical role in bringing the pandas to Atlanta. After playing several games of phone tag, we were able to schedule an interview. . . .

Although extremely intimidating, Dr. Maple was an oasis of information on everything related to the zoo, including the pandas. He described the acquisition of the pandas as "a long, arduous journey . . . very political and controversial. And we just persevered. We had to put forward a very honest and straightforward program of science and conservation. We thought we had the ability to do that. We had the people, we had the ideas, and we hoped we would have the resources" (Maple).

It was only after reading his book and scouring through various articles that I would thoroughly understand what he was talking about. . . . Maple had thought about acquiring pandas for the zoo when he first arrived in 1984. At that time it was very popular for American zoos to have pandas for a short period of time, such as three to six months, which was referred to as "rent-a-panda." He seriously began considering the idea in 1987, after the AZA (American Zoo and Aquarium Association) gave Zoo Atlanta a successful accreditation. Maple began making contact with Chinese officials through China Tech, an exchange program between China and Georgia Tech. He also sought the support of former President Jimmy Carter. Carter, who helped to restore full diplomatic relations with China during his presidency, agreed to assist the cause and made a request the next time he went to China (Maple 30). . . .

[From 1987 to 1994, Maple and his colleagues overcame a series of financial, humanitarian, and political objections by proposing a long-term loan arrangement that made the panda project more scientific and less commercial.]

Over the next year, Maple lobbied for greater support of the Chinese zoos. The zoos needed funds, and he was willing to do whatever it took to get the money. He asked Dr. Ulie Seal of the International Union of the Conservation of Nature to evaluate the panda situation and offer advice on how to support China. His conclusion, along with other evaluators, was that the conservation of pandas in China depended on both support in the wild and support in captivity. As a result of this report, the U.S. Fish and Wildlife Service eventually released revised regulations on panda imports in August of 1998. It became a breakthrough when the document was approved by the Chinese Association of Zoological Gardens. In the interview, Maple said, "Finally we got the zoo program a long-term loan. And now you can do it, if you get a long-term loan approved by our government that is conservation-oriented. And it is very difficult to do—very arduous. The cost of the pandas is now $1 million a year. Most zoos can't afford to do it" (Maple).

The San Diego Zoo was the first to benefit from the new AZA giant panda program, and they received their pandas in 1996. Atlanta became the next zoo in line to receive the animals. By 1998, Zoo Atlanta had worked in China for a year and developed a research plan. Everything was starting to fall into place, but there was another obstacle. Since the new program required a percentage of money to go to China, Zoo Atlanta had to find a field conservation program in China to give its funds to. After deciding on the Ministry of Forestry, Zoo Atlanta was ready to submit its request (Maple 38). On June 15, 1999, the application to import two giant pandas was approved by the U.S. Fish and Wildlife Service. . . .

The scheduled arrival time, however, kept getting pushed back due to many problems: final signatures, visas for the pilots, and landing rights approvals. . . . The day of departure, U.S. Senator Max Cleland was essential in getting the operation running punctually in China, through his influence in the U.S. Embassy in Beijing. Accompanying the pandas were Dr. Rita McManamon and two colleagues from China. There was no sleep during the entire 32-hour flight, which stopped in Anchorage, Alaska, to refuel. The veterinarians assessed the bears' health every twenty minutes, inspected them for dehydration and fatigue, and fed them bamboo. Meanwhile, in Atlanta, Maple recalled, "We could only worry and fuss, counting down the hours as they sped toward our reunion. Anytime a creature is translocated from one zoo to another, there is reason to plan and to worry." . . .

Thankfully, the pandas arrived on schedule without a scratch. . . . The panda exhibit opened on November 20, 1999, to a "euphoric reception" of media, visitors, scientists, and even a Chinese dance troupe (Maple 104). Zoo Atlanta found itself in the middle of "pandemonium" (Maple 43). . . .

The panda story was heard around the world. Companies such as Coca-Cola wanted to be a part of it. All the talk shows discussed it. Other zoos looked toward Zoo Atlanta for guidance on their own panda programs. . . .

The story of the pandas does not end here, however. It is only beginning. The breakthroughs Zoo Atlanta will be able to make in research and conservation are endless. . . .

My personal journey to knowing these wonderful animals has been extremely interesting and rewarding. After researching their long, complicated arrival, I see the pandas as so much more than a couple of cute bears. They are a symbol of how far Zoo Atlanta has come since 1984 [see Figure 11.2]. They are a symbol of how our city is slowly growing and expanding to an international level. Finally, they are a symbol of improved relations between the United States and China.

I feel a strong bond towards Lun-Lun and Yang-Yang, and they have, along with the rest of this project, completely changed my attitude towards zoos. It truly has been an eye-opening experience for me. A part of my youth has been recaptured. After experiencing that warm and fuzzy feeling from watching Lun-Lun and Yang-Yang, I developed a new sense of appreciation and wonder towards the zoo. And maybe this Sunday I'll be the one taking my dad to the zoo.

—Emily

Figure 11.2. Lun-Lun and Yang-Yang (pictured here) have adapted well to their new home at Zoo Atlanta. (Photo by Ashley Kruythoff.)

[Emily's paper included an impeccable works cited page. Her sources are included in the bibliography at the end of this book.]

Teacher Reflection

When I first started this project, I was an AP English teacher at Wheeler High School in Marietta, and I thought I couldn't find time to fit this worthwhile project into my course. As I reflect now on this assignment, I'm an AP U.S. history teacher at Grady High School in midtown Atlanta, and I still haven't found the time to fit this worthwhile project into my course. Because I'm closer to the zoo, and because I'm teaching the discipline best suited to oral history and local research, you'd think I'd have expanded this project, but I haven't. I'm too concerned about preparing my students for the College Board test in May to divert their attention. In making that decision, I'm reminded of the energy and enthusiasm that permeated my classroom when my students were acting a lot more like historians than history students. Students need the historical survey to understand the national community of which they are a part, and they also need assignments that encourage their true engagement in the community around them.

I know how hard it is to engage this process I am encouraging you to try, because in switching schools and subjects I lost my connection to it and have struggled mightily since to reengage it. Up against the clock and the calendar, I had hoped to complete a substantial community-based research project on Reconstruction during my first year at Grady, but I ultimately had to curtail my ambitions. The brief activity my students and I conducted that year (see Chapter 6, "A Correspondence between Atlanta Students") *was* valuable, but it lacked the substance and the scope of the Building Cities projects I had done while teaching American literature at my old school.

As had been the case when Meredith suggested the zoo as the site for my first Building Cities project, it was my students who reminded me why such projects are so important and ultimately worth whatever price you have to pay to fit them into your curriculum. My next encounter with the Building Cities theme didn't occur amid the coverage time crunch of my history class but rather during the deadline time crunch of my journalism class. Two seniors on my newspaper staff (Morgan and Rebecca) collaborated with a junior staff member (Dominick) to research, write, photograph, and design a center-spread feature documenting the Fourth Ward, a historic Atlanta neighborhood located in the part of the city served by our high school. The students initiated this assignment because they sought to document a place of great significance to their classmates, but they discovered that they had stumbled on a topic unbelievably rich in community themes. As a result, they organized their research into a fantastic three-story package: one chronicling the long history of the Fourth Ward, one explaining why Grady students who live in the Fourth Ward identify so strongly with their neighborhood, and one documenting and discussing gentrification in the neighborhood and anticipating what the future holds for it. Just as the students in Peggy Corbett's English class came to own their investigation of the Hickory Flat documentary, my students owned their reporting and writing on the Fourth Ward. The final product received first-place honors (in the diversity category) from the National Scholastic Press Association. The product and, more important, the process that led to it reveal how valuable community-themed work can be and how useful journalism can be in providing students an avenue to conduct that work.

My journalism students' success with research on the Fourth Ward prodded me to find a way to introduce community studies to my history students. When the opportunity presented itself, I seized it. Through my participation in the PEN/Faulkner Writers in Schools program, my students and I had the opportunity to study Tayari Jones's novel *Leaving Atlanta,* which is set in Atlanta in 1979 in the midst of what has become known as the Atlanta Child Murders. Our class read the novel, and students particularly enjoyed the author visit at the end of our study. The historical context that serves as the backdrop for the novel reenergized for me the theme of Building Cities. In researching the zoo and other urban institutions, my students and I have considered what we can learn about a city by researching what it elects to preserve. In this case, however, the question was reversed. What can we learn about a city by studying what it elects to forget?

From the summer of 1979 to the summer of 1981, twenty-nine black children, most of them elementary-age boys, were murdered in Atlanta. At first, city officials—among them the first black mayor and police chief in U.S. history—denied that the murders were related. After recanting this initial position, they created a task force that united several law enforcement agencies and ultimately led to the murder conviction of Wayne Williams, a young black man. Although he was only formally charged with two of the murders, the evidence in the trial and the public reaction to his conviction led many Atlantans to conclude that Williams had committed all of them. Other Atlantans—particularly those who lived in the areas where the murders occurred—still believe that Williams was a scapegoat who enabled Atlantans to move past this crisis and put an end to its damaging effect on the image of the city and its leaders.

I recalled that the murders were discussed briefly in Frederick Allen's *Atlanta Rising,* a book that had been central to the study of the Building Cities theme during the first KCAC summer institute. Revisiting the Allen book was my first move back to the materials and to the approach of KCAC teaching. My partner American studies teacher and I decided to use our reading of the novel *Leaving Atlanta* as an avenue to explore this tragic moment in the history of our city. The students conducted oral histories of Atlantans who remembered what it was like to live through that time. Some of the students interviewed their parents, but others were more ambitious. In the end, the impressive collection included interviews of local journalists who had covered the case, a prosecutor who brought the case against Williams, a private investigator hired by the parents of the victims, and several government officials who were running the city during the murders and the trial.

This project reinvigorated my commitment to studying community. I am excited to be back at work with students making history, not just studying it. Who knows, perhaps the collection of their oral histories will create the anthology I wished would mark the culmination of the Zoo Atlanta project outlined in this chapter. Whether or not we realize this goal, I and they will be the better for the experience.

Community ✤ Crossings

Suggestions on how you might adapt this lesson for a different classroom setting

- The instructional sequence suggests brainstorming techniques to identify significant cultural spaces in a city. These activities can be easily adapted to rural or suburban settings. A rural town might look at the buildings the town has elected to maintain and preserve, or how certain buildings may have been changed to facilitate a town's new focus, say from a mining town or a fishing village to a tourist destination. A suburban city might have transformed barns into wedding reception sites, libraries into restaurants, and forests into subdivisions. The project would work whether the site under investigation was as multileveled as the Atlanta zoo or as singular as a lighthouse on the coast.

12 "Writing Suburbia" in Pictures and Print

Sarah Robbins
Kennesaw State University, Kennesaw, Georgia

Overview

KCAC emphasizes writing as an avenue for learning, especially writing based on studying community culture. This assignment sought to blend two of our specific project principles—"Writing is a crucial tool for creating communities" (both inside the classroom and beyond) and "Authentic research is inquiry." I hoped my students would build a sense of classroom community and position themselves as participants in northwest Georgia culture by studying changes going on in the areas around us. More specifically, one of the most important objectives I had for this instructional sequence was for students to find and bring together several different kinds of materials/texts like those our class had been using to identify issues associated with changes in suburban life. We had read Kenneth Jackson's book *Crabgrass Frontier.* We had viewed two different video documentaries critiquing suburban life—*Sprawl* by CNN (a critique of unrestricted growth patterns) and *Displaced in the New South,* which explores the challenges facing immigrants in our region. We had discussed a number of newspaper articles, mainly identified by the students themselves from their reading of the *Atlanta Journal-Constitution.* (Fortunately, the *AJC* has a regular weekly insert on life in our suburban county, and the paper also runs regular features on issues such as the

> **School:** Kennesaw State University
> **City:** Kennesaw, Georgia
> **Grade level:** honors students at a regional state university with a commuter and residential student body
> **Discipline:** interdisciplinary seminar
> **School setting:** suburban
> **Number of students:** 12

Shifting Landscapes, Converging Peoples

internationalization of the suburbs.) A key aim I had for this assignment, after all that shared study, was to invite students to create their own interpretive texts by bringing together various ideas, questions, and findings they had generated about suburbia in an expressive form that capitalized on their ability to interpret visual text.

KCAC also assumes the following as one of our guiding principles: "proactive citizens recover, critique, and create community texts that reflect the dynamic values of local and larger communities." Therefore, one of my goals for this assignment was to have students gather visual data about the suburbs around the university and then create some interpretive frameworks for analyzing that data. I viewed the image gathering as a first step toward recovering some of the stories of change around us, and I hoped that seeing a range of images would highlight for all of us the shifting community values at work in our region, which has rapidly gone from rural to suburban. I hoped that my students might learn to look more critically at the elements of material and visual culture in their daily lives (e.g., road signs, shopping malls, subdivision designs). In addition, I hoped that their individual portrayals of suburban life might provide useful content for others interested in investigating those topics as well. (I had in mind both younger students in our region, who might not have the mobility my students do for taking pictures, but also students in other regions who might be able to compare and contrast their suburban communities with ours.)

Instructional Sequence

Early in this interdisciplinary seminar, we had viewed a documentary about how difficult it can be for immigrants coming to suburban communities in northwest Georgia to adapt to the local culture. Class discussion of the film included some insightful comments from students about the documentary's distinct point of view, which was often very critical of the prejudices some longtime residents were exhibiting toward immigrants. Students identified numerous examples of cinematic techniques (such as framing) and rhetorical strategies (such as editing/sequencing) to argue that the film often stereotyped longtime residents as insensitive and provincial. When my students' discussion crystallized around issues of framing and selection as crucial to critique of the documentary, I began to consider ways to pursue this interest further in later activities and assignments.

After I shared several newspaper articles from the *Atlanta Journal-Constitution,* a number of students began to bring in their own articles from the same paper and from suburban publications such as the *Marietta Daily Journal*. While I never gave a specific assignment asking students to find these materials, I did encourage them to continue the practice by giving up a few minutes of class time at the beginning of the period so that students could present such articles informally to the class. Often discussion of these pieces included comments about the photographs associated with the articles—where they were taken, how the photographer chose the subject, how the photo interacted with the print text of the article. (By then it was clear that this particular group of students really enjoyed thinking about images.)

I assigned Kenneth Jackson's *Crabgrass Frontier,* a sociological study of suburban life. We spent two class periods discussing the book, paying particular attention to ways in which conceptions of the suburbs have changed over time and to Jackson's thesis about the social values embedded in various suburban American lifestyles. (Teachers who cannot use the entire book might use excerpts.)

I then prepared an instruction sheet for the assignment and a model for the students to critique during one of our sessions in the computer lab.

Students had about a week to gather their images. Some students checked out digital cameras that were available through our project grant, but others used their own cameras. Since Kennesaw State students often have multiple responsibilities beyond attending school (jobs, families), I encouraged the whole class to share images so that students who did not have time to take photos themselves, or who were not successful in taking photographs of the caliber they wished, could draw on the class "bank" of suburban images. We created an archive of class photographs in digital form (as jpeg files), which I posted to a Web site location that class members could access.

During the second week, students drafted their projects and provided peer feedback. Finally, students presented their projects to the class audience. Several students ultimately chose to expand and revise their projects for the main project of the course.

Resources

See full directions for this assignment in the Classroom Resources section of the KCAC Web site, http://kcac.kennesaw.edu. Click on the bulleted item titled "University Honors Seminar—Interdisciplinary Course."

Student Artifact

See Heather's PowerPoint project, "Suburbia: Must we pave Paradise to Put up a Parkinglot?," at the following address: http://kcac. kennesaw.edu/thematic_content/shifting_landscapes_converging _peoples/shihome.html

Teacher Reflection

All of my students created interesting and worthwhile pieces for this assignment, and several of them continued to work on extended versions of the activity for their major course project. The enthusiasm they showed, and the quality of the work that many achieved, convinced me that I needed to bring more photography into my classroom, that I needed to allow more opportunities for linking personal-response writing with analytical writing, and that connecting relatively difficult scholarly texts to accessible materials from everyday life could enhance learning in my classroom.

Considering my students' success on this first try, if I were teaching the same class again I would bring their images and writing into the course sooner. Before we even began reading Jackson's book, I would ask students to bring in images or other photographs (of their own or from publications) they could interpret for the class. (As an alternative, I might use the activity described in Mimi Dyer's lesson in Chapter 3 as a warm-up, setting a foundation for the rest of the instructional sequence outlined here.) Then I would give students the assignment midway through our reading of the book, figuring that some might reuse the images they brought in early on, but that they would probably see the images quite differently based on our reading and discussion.

Community ✦ Crossings

Suggestions on how you might adapt this lesson for a different classroom setting

- Teachers could incorporate Gerri Hajduk's lesson, "Viewfinders: Students Picturing Their Communities" (Chapter 4), which explores how photographs enable students to study the past and present conditions of their communities.

- Another way of imagining how people lived in social groups is by sending or taking students to a cemetery. There they do a rubbing of a tombstone and write a first-person account of the community from the viewpoint of the dead person. This activity can be paired with Edgar Lee Masters's *Spoon River Anthology.*

- Suburban students can interview their parents about why they chose to reside in the suburbs rather than the city. They can also critically view films dedicated to suburban life, such as *American Beauty*, *Sunshine State*, and episodes of *The Simpsons*. Be sure to preview any film and follow your district's policy for approval and viewing.

- For directions about analyzing documents, photographs, cartoons, posters, maps, artifacts, sound recordings, and motion pictures, go to the U.S. National Archives & Records Administration (NARA) site: www.archives.gov/digital_classroom/lessons/analysis_worksheets/worksheets.html.

- The Library of Congress also has a wealth of resources, specifically about primary documents: http://memory.loc.gov/ammem/ndlpedu/lessons/psources/pshome.html.

Afterword and Action Plan

Diana Mitchell
Red Cedar Writing Project, Michigan State University, East Lansing

The work represented in this book celebrates the achievements of the teachers involved in Keeping and Creating American Communities. These lessons illustrate their commitment to broadening the way they view their teaching and to structuring learning activities that allow students to create new knowledge. The teachers' excitement about the learning their students were doing and their willingness to challenge their own teaching practices are apparent throughout.

Doing This Work in Your Classroom

This book is packed with concrete lessons that overflow with rich opportunities for students to be involved in their own learning. These lessons, which are inspirational and generative, make wonderful teaching models meant to be used. But the sheer immensity of these teachers' undertakings and the stunning variety of approaches and assignments can seem overwhelming. Readers might say, "This is all great, but what do I do with all this information?" To make your work easier, this afterword focuses on presenting the frames or questions around which many of these projects and assignments are based so that you can see ways to start this work in your own classroom. To begin to move these teaching approaches into your classroom:

- Work to use broader themes or questions to expand the way you frame your discipline in order to help students see the world in new ways.
- Build on what your students bring with them to the classroom.
- Create a classroom community in which all voices are listened to and collaboration is valued.

As you make these changes, do so gradually, trying out one piece at a time. If using broader themes seems too intimidating at first, for example, then focus on building on students' knowledge and experience. Many of the lessons in this book provide good, concrete ways to do this. Getting comfortable with constructing parts of your curriculum around student histories and interests is a great way to start enriching your teaching. As you build on student knowledge, have students share what they write or create with their peers in small groups. Organize group experiences such as having students analyze the games they played as children for cultural values embedded in the games. These kinds of activities build classroom community. As you see students' responses to this type of teaching, you may wish to begin to use some of the frames or questions suggested in the following section to bring your students even deeper into their own learning.

Using New Frames and Questions

Consider the following frames or approaches:

1. View underexamined histories as fruitful paths to critical literacy. Looking at the "untold" side of the story makes clear the existence of multiple points of view and the presence of power in every story/history told. What's the other side of the story? Who is given power to tell the story? What is important enough to photograph or write about? What would the people written about say about their portrayal? Dave Winter's students in "A Correspondence between Atlanta Students" (Chapter 6) and Peggy Corbett's in "Hometown History: The Hickory Flat Oral History Project" (Chapter 10) claimed the power to tell the untold story.

2. Notice that by "deconstructing" or taking apart the commonplace, such as our own neighborhoods and communities, these places can be examined for their cultural content. Who lived in this place before you did? Were any people removed against their will to make room for other people or structures? What evidence is there of the existence of these earlier people? What can you learn from the stores in your neighborhood or city? What can you learn from signs throughout your community, such as signs to subdivisions? What can you learn from the kinds of foods sold in grocery stores or from the number of churches/bars/schools/bookstores? How might the next generation view what this generation has built or destroyed in your community? Work at finding out the story behind the place you live. To see what such projects can look like, read Bonnie Webb's "Preserving the City" (Chapter 8) and Dave Winter's "My Classroom Really Is a Zoo" (Chapter 11).

3. Look at the world and all forms of media as your text, broadening your definition of *text* to include photographs, movies, songs, comics, and structures such as buildings, landscapes, and streets. Help

students "read" these texts to see what they can tell us about the culture. What can they "see into" this picture or photo? What do the objects mean or imply or tell us about the values of the culture? In "Viewfinders: Student Picturing Their Communities" (Chapter 4), Gerri Hajduk's students illustrate how much can be learned by looking carefully at photos.

4. Begin to see that artifacts/objects have multiple meanings which, when uncovered, provide insights into the multilayered nature of meaning. Houses, trees, stores can be looked at literally, symbolically, personally, politically, environmentally, culturally, literarily, or historically. The first piece in this book by Linda Stewart shows that trees can be personal, political (using trees for hanging), environmental (clear-cutting), cultural (trees that hold specific meaning for groups, such as the Liberty Tree and the Survivor Tree), poetic ("I Think That I Shall Never See a Poem as Lovely as a Tree"), literary (*The Giving Tree, A Tree Grows in Brooklyn*), and historical (trees that marked American Indian trails). By asking students to think about the motivation behind tree climbing, Stewart helps them understand the layers of meaning in everything that surrounds them, complicating the way they view the world. She takes the seemingly simple assignment of asking students to write about a time they climbed a tree and plumbs the depths of the experience, recognizing that everything in our society has cultural implications.

Other questions that fuel thinking and learning include:

- What can we learn about the identity of a culture, a society, a place, or even a person by examining what is chosen to preserve or keep?

- How do artifacts (businesses, sports teams, local heroes, authors, artists, churches, civic organizations, streets, local eccentrics) define a community? Look for hidden, ignored, or underlying components of the city.

- How do the concepts of "framing" (zoom shots, distance shots, what's given the most space) and "selection" (what's picked to be photographed or what's left out) have an impact on a movie, a documentary, or a book?

Building on Student Experience and Knowledge

Many of the lessons in this collection use student histories as the basis for assignments. Leslie Walker's "Making the Classroom Our Place" (Chapter 2) and Oreather Bostick-Morgan's "Giving Students a Penny for Their Thoughts" (Chapter 5) do just this. Lessons in this collection also help students see that they are a part of a place and a part of a culture by encouraging them to do some of the following:

1. Locate historical documents in your home (marriage certificates, birth certificates, deed or titles to land, insurance policies, wills, tax filings, award certificates). What could someone learn about your family from these documents in your home?

2. Deconstruct your home or your bedroom. How can you see culture at work in your personal life? Look at what you wear, eat, play, celebrate, cherish. What furnishings do you have, what fabrics, what's on your walls? What music is in your room? Work to uncover attitudes and values implicit in your selections.

3. Study your own life as history. What can you find out about societal, family, and community values by the way you live, the kind of school you attend, material objects in your life, emphasis on the spiritual, what you keep and collect?

4. Reflect on how you are related to your community (racially, economically, religiously, educationally, through family makeup). In which areas do you feel you are part of a majority? In which areas do you feel you are part of a minority? How do you experience these stances?

5. Create a documentary script about your class. What would you highlight? What would you leave out? If time and equipment are available, you could actually make the film. Then critique this documentary script or film. Does the whole class agree that the most important things were included? Do they feel any of the information only represented a minority of the class's view?

Recognizing What Is Needed to Succeed

Moving into this kind of teaching can be both exhilarating and frightening. The exhilaration comes from teachers knowing that students are connected to their learning. One teacher said, "When I stopped owning their learning experiences, they became true learners." But this kind of teaching can also provoke fear because teachers experience the sense of losing their center while they are shifting into a different way of framing their teaching and their practice.

Reading this book carefully, especially the teacher reflections, allows you to see that uncertainty and confusion accompany any new learning. Thus, when embarking on this kind of teaching, it helps to remember several things:

- We can teach only what we know how to do. If we cannot see how we are all located in a culture, cannot see that knowledge is constructed through someone's decision about what is important to include, cannot see that power eliminates many points of view while privileging others, then we cannot help students come to these understandings. By immersing themselves in learning and having models to get at this kind of learning, KCAC teachers could view their disciplines through cultural lenses, which they couldn't have done if they hadn't participated in the project training. Now that this group has broken the ground and left stories of their process in this collection, others can follow and adapt many of this group's approaches.

- We need support networks to help us maintain perspective. Part of real change involves losing our center, those feelings of security we have about what we teach, before we can find firm footing in the new. Since this kind of work takes support, it might be helpful to begin by asking a friend who may or may not teach in your building or district to become your learning buddy. Read parts of this publication together and discuss them as a way of starting your own network. Then try out some of the suggested frames or questions with one another until you feel you understand how to use them and are comfortable with the approach.

- We need to recognize that things take time. We can't produce significant change overnight. Teachers need sufficient time to participate in this kind of work because we are being asked to move out of our comfort zone.

So don't judge yourself for not moving fast enough. Implement changes, examine student response, and reflect on the learning and growth you see in student work before you proceed to another new challenge.

For further information and inspiration, visit the KCAC Web site at http://kcac.kennesaw.edu.

Bibliography

Edited by Stacie Janecki

Aldrich, Bess Streeter. *A Lantern in Her Hand.* 1928. New York: Puffin, 1997.

Allen, Frederick. *Atlanta Rising: The Invention of an International City, 1946–1996.* Atlanta: Longstreet, 1996.

American Beauty. Dir. Sam Mendes. Perf. Kevin Spacey and Annette Bening. 1999. Videotape. DreamWorks, 2000.

American Memory: Historical Collections for the National Digital Library. "The Learning Page: The Historian's Sources." 26 Sept. 2002. Library of Congress. 26 July 2003. <http://memory.loc.gov/ammem/ndlpedu/lessons/psources/pshome.html>.

Andrews, Raymond. *The Last Radio Baby: A Memoir.* Atlanta: Peachtree, 1990.

Ashton-Warner, Sylvia. *Teacher.* New York: Simon & Schuster, 1986.

Auster, Paul. "Auggie Wren's Christmas Story." *Fields of Reading: Motives for Writing.* 6th ed. Ed. Nancy R. Comley, et al. New York: Bedford/St. Martin's, 2001. 229–35.

Ayers, Rick. *Studs Terkel's* Working: *A Teaching Guide.* New York: New Press, 2001.

Ballenger, Bruce. *The Curious Researcher: A Guide to Writing Research Papers.* 3rd ed. Boston: Allyn and Bacon, 2001.

Baylor, Byrd. *When Clay Sings.* Illus. Tom Bahti. New York: Aladdin, 1972.

Black Elk. *Black Elk Speaks: Being the Life Story of a Holy Man of the Oglala Sioux, as Told to John G. Neihardt.* New York: W. Morrow, 1932.

Bridging the Gap: Moving Stories of Georgia. Ed. Peter Difazio and Sprayberry High School VOX Staff. Kennesaw, GA: Kennesaw Mountain Writing Project, 2001.

Brown, Chandler. "Senior Couple to Sell Last Farm in DeKalb." *Atlanta Journal Constitution* 21 Jan. 2002: D1 & D2.

Brown, Cynthia Stokes. *Like It Was: A Complete Guide to Writing Oral History.* New York: Teachers and Writers Collaborative, 1988.

Brown, Jennifer. "Africa and the Caribbean." *Ain't I a Woman! A Book of Women's Poetry from around the World.* Ed. Illona Linthwaite. New York: Peter Bedrick, 1990. 35.

Brown, Marc. *Arthur Writes a Story.* Boston: Little, Brown, 1996.

Bruchac, Joseph. *The First Strawberries: A Cherokee Story.* Illus. Anna Vojtech. New York: Dial, 1993.

————. *The Journal of Jesse Smoke: A Cherokee Boy.* New York: Scholastic, 2001.

Carter, Jimmy. *Always a Reckoning, and Other Poems.* New York: Times Books, 1995.

————. *An Hour before Daylight: Memories of a Rural Boyhood.* New York: Simon & Schuster, 2001.

Cather, Willa Sibert. *My Ántonia.* 1918. New York: Houghton Mifflin, 1995.

Cleary, Beverly. *Ramona Quimby, Age 8.* Illus. Alan Tiegreen. New York: Dell, 1988.

Conley, Robert J. *Mountain Windsong: A Novel of the Trail of Tears.* Norman: University of Oklahoma Press, 1992.

Cutrer, Emily Fourmy. "Visualizing Nineteenth-Century American Culture." *American Quarterly* 51.4 (1999): 896.

"Daryl Cagle's Professional Cartoonists Index." *MSN Slate Magazine.* Microsoft Corporation. 26 July 2003 <http://cagle.slate.msn.com>.

Deedy, Carmen Agra. *Growing Up Cuban in Decatur, Georgia: Stories Created and Told by Carmen Agra Deedy.* Audiocassette. Atlanta: Peachtree, 1995.

Evans, Mari. "Modern American Suite in Four Movements." *A Dark and Splendid Mass.* New York: Harlem River Press, 1992. 2–7.

Fitzgerald, David G., and Robert J. Conley. *Cherokee.* Portland, OR: Graphic Arts Center, 2002.

Fitzgerald, F. Scott. *The Great Gatsby.* 1925. New York: Scribner, 1995.

Fleischman, Paul. *Seedfolks.* Illus. Judy Pedersen. New York: HarperCollins, 1997.

Frost, Robert. "Mending Wall." *The Norton Anthology of Poetry.* 1st ed. Ed. Arthur M. Eastman. New York: W. W. Norton, 1970. 908.

"F. Scott Fitzgerald: The Great American Dreamer." Prod. History Television Productions. Videotape. A&E Home Video, 1977.

Galphin, Bruce. "At Omni International, Fantasy & Dreams Become Reality." *Atlanta Magazine* May 1976: 41–43, 98, 118.

————. "The Kroffts Create a World." *Atlanta Magazine* July 1974: 46–48.

Gifford, Kathie Lee. *Heart of a Woman.* CD. Universal, 2000.

Ginsberg, Allen. "America." *The Heath Anthology of American Literature.* 2nd ed. Ed. Paul Lauter. Lexington, MA: D. C. Heath, 1994. 2386–388.

Glancy, Diane. *Pushing the Bear: A Novel of the Trail of Tears.* San Diego: Harcourt, Brace, 1996.

Golden Ink. "About North Georgia." 12 Oct. 2002 <www.ngeorgia.com/history/nghisttt.html>.

Gone with the Wind. Dir. Victor Fleming. Perf. Clark Gable, Vivien Leigh, Olivia de Havilland, and Leslie Howard. Metro-Goldwyn-Mayer, 1939.

The Great Gatsby. Dir. Jack Clayton. Prod. David Merrick. Paramount, 1974.

Gruchow, Paul. "What a Garden Can Teach Us." *Grass Roots: The Universe of Home.* Minneapolis: Milkweed Editions, 1995. 77–80.

Guterson, David. "No Place Like Home: On the Manicured Streets of a Master-Planned Community. *Seeing and Writing.* Ed. Donald McQuade and Christine McQuade. New York: Bedford/St. Martin's, 2000. 88–94.

Guthrie, Woody. "This Land Is Your Land." *American Favorite Ballads.* New York: Oak, 1961. 30. [print version]

———. "This Land Is Your Land." *This Land is Your Land.* The Asch Recordings, Vol. 1. CD. Smithsonian Folkways, 1997.

Hawkins, Ted. "You're Beautiful to Me." *Love You Most of All: More Songs from Venice Beach.* CD. Evidence Music, 1998.

Hayden, Dolores. *The Power of Place: Urban Landscapes as Public History.* Cambridge: MIT Press, 1995.

Heard, Georgia. *Awakening the Heart: Exploring Poetry in Elementary and Middle School.* Portsmouth, NH: Heinemann, 1999.

Hendrick, Bill. "The Bear Necessities: Compound Gives Pair All the Comforts of Home and More." *Atlanta Journal and Constitution* 2 Nov. 1999: D1.

Howard, Elizabeth Fitzgerald. *Aunt Flossie's Hats (and Crab Cakes Later).* Reprint ed. New York: Clarion Books, 1995.

"H. R. Pufnstuf: The Strange World of Sid and Marty Krofft." *E! True Hollywood Story.* Prod. Andrew Swift. Videocassette. E! Entertainment Television, 2000.

Hughes, Langston. "I, Too." *The Harper American Literature.* 2nd ed., vol. 2. Ed. Donald McQuade. New York: HarperCollins, 1993. 1478.

Hurston, Zora Neale. *Their Eyes Were Watching God.* 1937. Urbana: University of Illinois Press, 1978.

Jackson, Kenneth T. *Crabgrass Frontier: The Suburbanization of the United States.* New York: Oxford University Press, 1985.

Jeffers, Robinson. "Shine, Perishing Republic." *The Norton Anthology of American Literature.* 4th ed., vol. 2. Ed. Nina Baym et al. New York: Norton, 1994. 1242–243.

Jones, Tayari. *Leaving Atlanta.* New York: Warner, 2002.

Kilmer, Joyce. "Trees." *Modern American Poetry: An Introduction.* Ed. Louis Untermeyer. New York: Harcourt, Brace and Howe, 1919. 119.

Knowles, John. *A Separate Peace.* 1959. New York: Scribner, 1996.

Lewis, Deborah Shaw, and Gregg Lewis. *"Did I Ever Tell You about When Your Grandparents Were Young?"* Grand Rapids, MI: Zondervan, 1994.

The Life and Times of Willie B. Prod. C. B. Hackworth and Kevin Caffrey. WSB-TV and Zoo Atlanta, 2001.

Lyon, George Ella. "Where I'm From." *The United States of Poetry*. Prod. Joshua Blum and Bob Holman. Dir. Mark Pellington. Videocassette. Washington Square Films, 1996.

———. "Where I'm From." 12 Oct. 2002 <www.bright.net/~dlackey/ wherefrom.pdf>.

Macrorie, Ken. *The I-Search Paper*. Portsmouth, NH: Boynton/Cook, Heinemann, 1988.

Maple, Terry L. *Saving the Giant Panda*. Atlanta: Longstreet, 2000.

Mayer, Ben, et al. "The Lost World of Sid and Marty Krofft." *The Catalyst* 26 April 2001: 16–17, 25.

McKay, Claude. "America." *The New Cavalcade: African American Writing from 1760 to the Present*. Vol. 1. Ed. Arthur P. Davis, J. Saunders Redding, and Joyce Ann Joyce. Washington, DC: Howard University Press, 1991. 445–46. [This poem is also available in the following sources: Claude McKay, "America," *Elements of Literature: Literature of the United States with Literature of the Americas*, fifth course, ed. Robert Probst, Austin: Holt, Rinehart, and Winston, 199, p. 744; *The Heath Anthology of American Literature*, 2nd ed., ed. Paul Lauter, Lexington, MA: D. C. Heath, 1994, p. 1693.]

McQuade, Donald, and Christine McQuade. "Coming to Terms with Place." *Seeing and Writing*. Boston: Bedford/St. Martin's, 2000. 68–108.

Mitchell, Margaret. *Gone with the Wind*. 1936. New York: Warner Books, 1993.

Morgan, Norah, and Juliana Saxton. *Asking Better Questions*. Markham, Ontario: Pembroke, 1994.

Morrison, Toni. *Beloved*. 1987. New York: A. A. Knopf, 1998.

NARA Digital Classroom. "Document Analysis Worksheets." 26 July 2003. The National Archives and Records Administration. 26 July 2003 <www.archives.gov/digital_classroom/lessons/analysis_worksheets /worksheets.html>.

Nolte, Carl. "A Roaring Decade, a Glorious New City, a Rival to the South: Back on Its Feet after the Big Earthquake and Fire, San Francisco Built Up Muni, Grabbed Water and Partied with Mayor Sunny Jim Rolph— until the Crash of '29." *San Francisco Chronicle* 25 April 1999, Sunday sect. 1.

Paulsen, Gary. *Nightjohn*. 1993. New York: Laurel Leaf, 1995.

Presenting the UPS Panda Express. "Track the Pandas." United Parcel Service. 20 May 2001 <http://www.pandaexpress.ups.com/track/ track.html>.

Purdue University Online Writing Lab. "Research and Documenting Sources." 2 May 2002. Purdue University. 6 June 2002 <http:// owl.english.purdue.edu/handouts/research/index.html>.

Reagon, Bernice Johnson, and Toshi Reagon. "Your Country." *Africans in*

America: America's Journey through Slavery. Soundtrack of WGBH/TV-PBS documentary, WGBH Educational Foundation, 1998.

Russell, Adam. *Where the Deer Ran: Events Leading to the Cherokee Removal.* Kennesaw, GA: Kennesaw Mountain Writing Project, 2001.

Sandburg, Carl. "Chicago." *The Harper American Literature.* 2nd ed., vol. 2. Ed. Donald McQuade et al. New York: HarperCollins, 1993. 1266–267.

Sanders, Scott Russell. "Homeplace." *Seeing and Writing.* Ed. Donald McQuade and Christine McQuade. Boston: Bedford/St. Martin's, 2000. 101–5.

"San Francisco in the '20s." *Bay Area 2000.* Prod. and dir. KRON-TV. KRON-TV, San Francisco, 2000.

Silverstein, Shel. *The Giving Tree.* 1964. New York: HarperCollins, 1999.

———. *A Light in the Attic.* 1981. New York: HarperCollins, 1996.

———. *Where the Sidewalk Ends: The Poems and Drawings of Shel Silverstein.* New York: HarperCollins, 1974.

Simon, Paul. "America." *Live Rhymin'.* 1974. CD. Warner Bros., 1990. [Also available on *Simon and Garfunkel's Greatest Hits.* 1972. CD. Sony, 1990.]

Smith, Betty. *A Tree Grows in Brooklyn.* 1943. New York: Perennial Classics, 2001.

Smoke. Dir. Wayne Wang. Perf. Harvey Keitel and William Hurt. 1995. Videotape. Buena Vista, 1996.

Sneve, Virginia Driving Hawk. *The Cherokees.* Illus. Ronald Himler. New York: Holiday House, 1996.

Spinelli, Jerry. *Maniac Magee.* Boston: Little, Brown, 1990.

Stauffer, Russell G. *Directing the Reading-Thinking Process.* New York: Harper & Row, 1975.

"Symbols: Tribes of the American Indian Nation." Chart. Phoenix: Jayhawk, 1998.

Taylor, Ron. "Can Pandas Bear Atlanta Autumn? Warm Weather Worries Officials from China during Tour of Zoo." *Atlanta Journal and Constitution* 4 Nov. 1987: A23.

Terkel, Studs. *Working: People Talk about What They Do All Day and How They Feel about What They Do.* New York: New Press, 1997.

Twain, Mark. *The Adventures of Huckleberry Finn.* Ed. John D. Seelye. New York: Penguin, 1986.

Vergara, Camilo Jose. "Photographs of 65 East 125th Street, Harlem" [12 photographs]. *Seeing and Writing.* Ed. Donald McQuade and Christine McQuade. Boston: Bedford/St. Martin's, 2000. 89–99.

Wallis, Michael. "Searching for Hidden Rhythms in Twilight Land." *Way Down Yonder in the Indian Nation: Writings from America's Heartland.* New York: St. Martin's Griffin, 1997. 2–17.

Walls, Carrie P. "Children's Exchange." *Spelman Messenger* (November 1886): 6.

Warner, Jack. "'Rent-a-Panda' Flap May Mean Double Trouble for Atlanta." *Atlanta Journal and Constitution* 23 June 1988: A1.

Welty, Eudora. "The Little Store." *Seeing and Writing.* Ed. Donald McQuade and Christine McQuade. Boston: Bedford/St. Martin's, 2000. 78–83.

Wheatley, Nadia. *My Place.* Illus. Donna Rawlins. Brooklyn: Kane/Miller, 1992.

Whitman, Walt. "I Hear America Singing." *The Poetry of Walt Whitman.* Long Island Globalink. 1995. 12 Oct. 2002 <www.liglobal.com/walt/i-hear-america.html>.

Wiesel, Elie. *Night.* Trans. Stella Rodway. New York: Bantam, 1982.

"World Newspapers, Magazines, and News Sites in English." World-Newspapers.com. 30 July 2003 <www.world-newspapers.com>.

Zinsser, William. *On Writing Well: The Classic Guide to Writing Nonfiction.* New York: HarperResource Quill, 2001.

Zoo Atlanta. "Panda Cam." Zoo Atlanta. 17 Mar 2001 <http://www.zooatlanta.org/pandacam.html>. [Now available at "The Animals: Georgia's Panda Project." www.zooatlanta.org/site/the_animals/giant_panda_info.html.]

Zoo Atlanta. Brochure on pandas. 17 Apr. 2001.

"Zoo Atlanta Issue." *Atlanta History: A Journal of Georgia and the South* 43 (Winter 2000).

Editors

Sarah Robbins, director of KCAC, is author of *Managing Literacy, Mothering America: Women's Narratives on Reading and Writing in the Nineteenth Century.* A former K–12 teacher, Robbins co-directed two earlier NEH-funded curriculum programs: Domesticating the Secondary Canon and Making American Literatures. With Mimi Dyer, she coedited *Writing America: Classroom Literacy and Public Engagement.* Robbins has won regional and national awards for scholarship on teaching, American literature, and the role of literature in nineteenth-century U.S. culture.

Dave Winter is KCAC print publications coordinator. After nine years of teaching at Wheeler High School in Marietta, Georgia, he joined the staff of Atlanta's Henry W. Grady High School, where he teaches journalism and U.S. history and advises the student newspaper. Winter was the Georgia associate director of the NWP's Making American Literatures Institute in 1998. His publications include essays in *Making American Literatures in High School and College,* the NWP's *The Quarterly,* the Organization of American Historians' *Magazine of History, The English Record,* and *Kentucky English Bulletin.*

Contributors

The following list includes members of the Keeping and Creating American Communities project team who contributed lesson plans, assisted with editing, and/or wrote material for the Community Crossings boxes within chapters.

Judy Bebelaar, a teacher in public schools in San Francisco since 1967, is now retired. She is a Bay Area Writing Project (California) teacher-consultant and former president of the board of California Poets in the Schools. Recent publications are "Kien: Learning to Write in a Second Language" in *Meeting the Challenges: Stories from Today's Classrooms* and "Hear Our Voices," an article about student concerns as expressed in poetry across generations, in the *San Francisco Examiner Magazine.*

Sharon Bishop is a secondary English teacher with twenty-three years of experience at the same rural Nebraska school, where she developed a course called Nebraska Literature/Composition: A Sense of Place. Co-director for the Nebraska Writing Project, Bishop participated in Rural Voices, Country Schools, sponsored by NWP and the Annenberg Rural Challenge. *Rural Voices: Place-Conscious Education and the Teaching of Writing* includes Sharon's chapter "A Sense of Place." She has received an Exemplary Classroom Award from Foxfire and has been awarded the Nebraska Writing Project's Teacher of the Year Award.

Traci Blanchard, a National Writing Project teacher-consultant since 1997, is technology coordinator for KCAC. Teaching world literature and Advanced Placement English language and composition at Lassiter High School, she also serves as the yearbook sponsor, writing lab manager, school Webmaster, and "technology guru" for her language arts department. Other Web sites she has designed include a secondary language arts site for the Cobb County school district and *The Writing Room,* an online literary magazine.

Oreather J. Bostick-Morgan, a speech language pathologist with Atlanta Public Schools, received her master's degree from Tennessee State University. She is co-director of the Peachtree Urban Writing Project. This twenty-two-year veteran educator was selected as 2001–2002 Teacher of the Year for Atlanta Public Schools. She periodically serves as adjunct professor at Clark Atlanta University.

Landon A. Brown II is a teacher and administrator at Lindley Middle School. He graduated from Georgia State University and Mercer University and has a master's degree in middle grades education. Brown has presented at conferences held by the National Council of Teachers of Mathematics.

Peggy Maynard Corbett is team leader of KCAC's Cultivating Homelands strand. A secondary English teacher in rural Cherokee County, Georgia, for thirteen years, she is now a teacher on special assignment for her school system, helping teachers to develop classroom resources and curricula, including community studies projects. She earned her master of arts in professional writing at Kennesaw State University in 2003.

Mimi Dyer is co-director of KCAC and coordinator of the Advanced Science, Mathematics and Technology Academy at Kennesaw Mountain High School. A graduate of Duke University and recipient of a master's in professional writing from Kennesaw State University, she is currently enrolled in a doctoral program for educational leadership. A National Board Certified Teacher, Dyer is an active teacher-researcher, and she co-edited *Writing America: Classroom Literacy and Public Engagement* with Sarah Robbins. Her article about anthologizing American literature with students appears in *Making American Literatures in High School and College.*

Gerri Hajduk is team leader for KCAC's Shifting Landscapes, Converging Peoples strand. She has taught Advanced Placement U.S. history, American studies, and honors world history for over twenty years at Wheeler High School in Marietta, Georgia. Hajduk has participated in NEH-funded curriculum development projects such as Domesticating the Secondary Canon and Making American Literatures.

Patsy Hamby is a language arts teacher at Hiram High School in Paulding County, Georgia, and a part-time faculty member at Kennesaw State University. A graduate of Kennesaw State who also holds a master of arts in professional writing from KSU, Hamby was a 1994 founding fellow of the Kennesaw Mountain Writing Project. She has been named Teacher of the Year at Hiram High School and a member of Who's Who among America's Teachers.

Barbara Wooden Howry is a KCAC pilot teacher representing the Oklahoma State University Writing Project (OSUWP). She works at Putnam City West, an urban high school in Oklahoma City, where she teaches English and creative writing. As a result of her work for KCAC, Howry and OSUWP received an NWP minigrant for Oklahoma teachers to bring the work of community studies to their students.

Ed Hullender is co-leader of the Educating for Citizenship team for KCAC. A high school world history teacher for over twenty years, Hullender is active in improving the quality of social studies instruction in the Cobb County school system. He is a graduate of Jacksonville State University with an EdS in history.

Stacie Janecki is a 2002 graduate of Kennesaw State University, where she majored in English with a concentration in creative writing. She currently works as program coordinator for the KCAC program and for the Kennesaw Mountain Writing Project.

Bernadette Lambert, KCAC performance coordinator, has worked as a literacy specialist for Cobb County middle and elementary schools. An NWP teacher-consultant since 1996, Lambert held leadership roles with NWP's Project Outreach and Making American Literatures initiatives. She earned her master of arts in professional writing from Kennesaw State and has won the KMWP's Sponsor of Literacy Award for community leadership. Her publications include a short story in *Teaching Powerful Writing* and articles in journals such as NWP's *The Quarterly*.

Amy Meadows is a freelance writer and president of Green Meadows Communications, LLC, a firm specializing in feature writing and corporate marketing literature. Her writing credits include contributions to *Real Estate Executive Magazine, Builder/Architect, CE News, The Structural Engineer, The Magnolia, Cherokee Living, North Fulton Living, The AutoPILOT,* and *Points North*.

Deborah J. Mitchell is co-leader of KCAC's Educating for Citizenship team. She is co-director of the Peachtree Urban Writing Project. Mitchell is a graduate of Spelman College and holds a master's degree in special education from Columbus State University. She is a fourteen-year veteran of the Atlanta Public School system, where she is a fifth-grade teacher at T. H. Slater Elementary School.

Diana Mitchell serves on the KCAC National Advisory Board. A former co-director of the Red Cedar Writing Project at Michigan State University, she has been a member of NCTE's Secondary Section Steering Committee, chair of NCTE's Women in Literacy and Life Assembly, chair of NCTE's Assembly on Literature for Adolescents (ALAN), president of the Michigan Council of Teachers of English, and editor of *Language Arts*. She recently published *Children's Literature: An Invitation to the World*.

Diane J. Shearer currently teaches Pre-Advanced Placement American literature and composition, AP language and composition, and journalism at Chamblee High School. She holds a master's degree from the University of Georgia. Shearer serves as a teacher-consultant for the College Board, training other teachers in Pacesetter English and the Pre-Advanced Placement model curriculum. Her writing has appeared in publications such as *The International Railway Traveler, English Journal,* and *Teaching Tolerance*.

Sylvia Martinez Spruill is a teacher participant in KCAC's Shifting Landscapes, Converging Peoples strand. She is a graduate of Agnes Scott College, where she received a bachelor's degree in English and a master of arts in teaching. A National Board certified instructor, she teaches Pacesetter English and Advanced Placement literature and composition at Campbell High School.

Linda Hadley Stewart was pilot teacher coordinator for KCAC. A full-time instructor at Kennesaw State University, she teaches world literature and composition courses. At the University of New Hampshire, she earned a master of arts in teaching and a master of arts in English literature. She has secondary school experience teaching a varied curriculum ranging from at-risk to honors English for a diverse student population.

Linda Templeton has worked with the Cultivating Homelands research team and helped coordinate workshops associated with the KCAC project. A graduate of Kennesaw State University, she began her NWP participation in 1995 with the Making American Literatures project. Templeton has also worked on a Rural Sites Network project funded by an NWP minigrant. She teaches ninth-grade English at Cartersville High School in Georgia.

Rozlyn T. Truss is a fourth-grade teacher at Williams Elementary School in Atlanta. She received her BA in early childhood education from Clark Atlanta University and her master of arts in professional writing from Kennesaw State. Truss has taught grades 3 through 5 and has worked as a learner support strategist. She was a 1998 fellow of the Kennesaw Mountain Writing Project and a 2001 fellow of that NWP site's advanced institute.

Leslie M. Walker serves KCAC as team leader for the Reclaiming Displaced Heritages strand. She received her bachelor's degree in secondary English education and a master's in professional writing from Kennesaw State University. She has been a teacher of ninth-, tenth-, and twelfth-grade English at Campbell High School in Smyrna, Georgia, for over eight years. Walker was a fellow of the KMWP's 1998 invitational summer institute and the 1999 advanced institute on teachers' professional writing.

Bonnie G. Webb is KCAC's team leader for the Building Cities strand. She has taught social studies, science, and language arts to gifted middle school students and currently works at Cooper Middle School in Austell, Georgia. Bonnie is a graduate of Bloomsburg University of Pennsylvania and holds a master's in middle grades education from Kennesaw State. Bonnie has received technology grants from the U S West Foundation, Media One, Georgia Supporters of the Gifted, Educating for a Sustainable Future, and NWP.

This book was typeset in Palatino, Futura, and Helvetica
by Electronic Imaging.
The typefaces used on the cover were Trebuchet and Garamond Book Condensed.
The book was printed on 60-lb. Williamsburg Offset paper by Versa Press, Inc.